W9-BYH-109

Strategy Pure and Simple

How Winning CEOs Outthink Their Competition

Michel Robert

McGraw-Hill, Inc.

New York San Francisco Washington, D.C. Auckland Bogotá
Caracas Lisbon London Madrid Mexico City Milan
Montreal New Delhi San Juan Singpore
Sydney Tokyo Toronto

Library of Congress Cataloging-in-Publication Data

Robert, Michel.
    Strategy pure and simple : how winning CEOs outthink their
competition / Michel Robert.
        p.   cm.
    Includes index.
    ISBN 0-07-053131-5
    1. Strategic planning—United States.   2. Competition,
International.   3. Success in business—United States.   4. Chief
executive officers—United States.   I. Title.
HD30.28.R634   1993
658.4′012—dc20   92-23176
                                                                          CIP

Copyright © 1993 by Michel Robert. All rights reserved. Printed in the
United States of America. Except as permitted under the United States
Copyright Act of 1976, no part of this publication may be reproduced or
distributed in any form or by any means, or stored in a data base or re-
trieval system, without the prior written permission of the publisher.

          8 9 0   DOC/DOC   9 8 7 6 5

ISBN   0-07-053131-5

*The sponsoring editor for this book was Betsy N. Brown, the editing supervisor
was Jane Palmieri, and the production supervisor was Donald Schmidt. It was
set in Palatino by McGraw-Hill's Professional Book Group composition unit.*

Printed and bound by R. R. Donnelley & Sons Company.

 This book is printed on recycled, acid free paper containing a minimum of 50% recycled de-
inked fiber.

Contents

Foreword

You may have read many books on strategy, but Mike Robert brings a new voice and a provocative point of view to the subject.

First, as he declares, his concepts were developed not in academe but in the boardrooms of major corporations. They have been used in the real world by real executives operating real companies, not only in the United States but also in a number of other countries.

Second, Mike Robert notes that his concepts are simple yet powerful. As he puts it, "They make sense and, when applied, bring immediate results that breed consensus and direction—something not easy to achieve in any organization."

Third, the book cites many examples of successful CEOs and companies that are using his strategic concepts to gain competitive advantage and produce above average results.

Altogether, this book represents the thinking and experience of a man who has more than 15 years' experience working with more than 230 corporations around the globe. Change is the only certainty that we face in the challenging years ahead, and Mike Robert gives us his insights on how to effect constructive change.

Marshall Loeb
Managing Editor
Fortune *Magazine*

Preface

The United States, in the last 30 years, has lost big chunks of its markets to so-called foreign competition. Yet, this has occurred during a period when U.S. corporations have been engrossed more than ever before in concepts of "strategic" planning. Why has this decline in market share occurred? One would think that such concepts would have resulted in making the companies that practiced them more competitive. However, the result has been the exact opposite. One, therefore, needs to question the validity of such concepts.

Strategy Pure and Simple does precisely that. It shows that U.S. companies following such techniques are losing ground because these "miracle" recipes are conceptually flawed and based on "ivory tower" analysis.

Unlike Michael Porter, who claims to have developed his concepts of competitive analysis while having spent "seven and a half years in the Harvard Business School library," the process of Strategic Thinking described here is the result of 15 years of work with the CEOs and the management teams of over 230 companies worldwide. In other words, I have been in the "war room" with these CEOs while they were trying to formulate and articulate their strategy for their companies. The process of Strategic Thinking described in this book reflects the thought process that successful CEOs employ to engage their employees in a winning vision and strategy that beats the competition.

The thrust of this book is that U.S. companies are being "out-thunked." As stated in an article appearing in the July 8, 1991, issue of *Forbes*, the ex-chairman of Ford Europe expressed it best when he said: "We are engaging in the Third World War. This one won't be won by Schwarzkopf or some other fellow who looks good on TV. It's going to be won by [someone] who can think."

I couldn't agree more. After 15 years of working closely with the CEOs and the management teams of over 230 major corporations worldwide, I am convinced that America's lack of strategic thinking skill is at the root of its problem. The reason is simple. For most of this century, there was no need to think strategically! American companies could do no wrong. Blessed with a large portion of the world's resources, an enterprising population, and in contrast with the devastation of most of Europe and Asia in two world wars, by 1955 the United States accounted for 75 percent of the world's GNP! Why? No competition. There is no great need to think strategically under such circumstances.

Furthermore, U.S. companies had at their doorstep the largest consumer market in the world. Exports were, for U.S. companies, considered as "incremental" business. Unfortunately, that is still the same for too many U.S. firms. As a result, most executives of U.S. companies are operationally competent but strategically deficient. In other words, when the focus of a business is strictly limited to keeping up with an ever-increasing demand for its products, operational skills alone suffice to breed success. All that changed with the advent of the Japanese and the Europeans, particularly the Germans.

The work of DPI has found that two key elements breed strategic skills in management executives:

- The lack of, or diminishing, resources
- Business conducted outside your own domestic boundaries

Restricted resources exert pressure on management to allocate resources more carefully and necessitate the need to think more strategically. Doing business outside your natural habitat places the enterprise in unfamiliar terrain where the rules of the game are different and, thus, creates a need for the company to think strategically in its allocation of resources and pursuit of opportunities.

The Germans, Japanese, Swedes, Dutch, and a few others have

had these two constraints working against them much longer (1000 years) than their U.S. counterparts, so their skills of strategic thinking are more sharply developed.

Almost all CEOs of publicly traded companies in the United States have told me that the biggest impediment to sound strategic thinking is Wall Street's thirst for increases in quarterly earnings. This is pure fallacy. In fact, if one talks to investment fund managers, they say the exact opposite. Their complaint is that most CEOs focus too much on the short term and do not have a longer-term strategy. They will even show you graphs and charts proving that investment managers who move their money around each quarter based on the ups and downs of the firm's quarterly earnings have not performed as well as those that have invested for the longer term. A case in point is Warren Buffet's firm, Berkshire Hathaway, which has consistently invested for the longer term since its inception and which has outperformed most of the investment houses that shuffle their portfolios each quarter. Furthermore, there is a movement afoot by several fund managers to get more involved on company boards in an attempt to force better strategic thinking on the CEOs of the firms in which they invest.

Such a movement is currently afoot at Sears, once America's largest and best managed retailers and now second to Wal-Mart. Dale Hanson, the manager of the California Public Employees Retirement System (the country's largest public pension fund), has recently been agitating to replace the Sears board in order to force its CEO to develop a better long-term strategy for the business. Although CalPERS has only 0.6 percent of Sears' stock, it still prefers this option as opposed to simply moving its investment to another company. So much for the short-term orientation of shareholders!

Further evidence that there is no relationship between Wall Street and a CEO's inability to think strategically was presented in a study done by Randall Woolridge and Charles Snow, reprinted in the Appendix. Their conclusion: Stock market gyrations have no impact on a CEO's ability to think or invest for the long-term benefit of the corporation.

America's passion with flawed concepts of planning that view a corporation strictly as a financial model to be tweaked and twisted in a variety of preprogrammed formulas in order to increase "shareholder value" has turned most of our CEOs into accountants rather than leaders and strategists. In a lecture to the Royal Society in London on February 6, 1992, Akio Morita, CEO of Sony, perhaps one of the world's most successful companies since World War II, remarked:

> In Japan you will notice that most every major manufacturer is run by an engineer or technologist. Someone once mentioned to me that many U.S. and U.K. companies are headed by chartered accountants. This strikes me as very curious. Though I have a great deal of respect for accountants and financial professionals, I do not believe they should be at the helm of industry. For an accountant, the central concern is statistics and figures—of *past* performance. So how can an accountant reach and grab the future if he is always looking at last quarter's results? Just as you would not have a football coach who never played the game, how can someone who does not understand the workings of technology take the reins of a manufacturing operation?

I am in complete agreement. And the thrust of this book is around leadership and strategy. With the changes that are happening all around the world, the ability to think strategically in order to formulate and articulate a clear vision accompanied by succinct strategic goals and objectives will be a critical skill needed by CEOs who want to be successful in the years to come. Organizations will hold together, and their people will follow those leaders who can clearly state where they are leading the company.

Our thesis is that there is little strategic thinking in many U.S. companies today because there has not been a need for it. As a result, most executives of U.S. companies have developed very effective operational skills but have not become very adept at strategic skills. As such, our mission for the last 15 years has been to uncover the process and the skills of strategy that successful CEOs use to outthink their competition.

Good reading.

Michel Robert

1

Fire, Ready, Aim: The Best Way to Lose the Game!

"Fire, ready, aim!," as claimed by Tom Peters and Bob Waterman in their mega hit *In Search of Excellence* of the early 1980s, was a key characteristic of the most successful American companies they had apparently surveyed. Now a decade later, the majority of the so-called most successful companies, according to these two gentlemen, are in worse market positions than they were back then. If "fire, ready, aim!" is a trait of successful companies, then why are they less successful 10 years later? Pity American industry if this "key to success" continues to be the underlying philosophy of American management. In fact, our 20 years of work with over 300 companies worldwide has convinced us that this kind of approach to management is the *cause* of America's competitive decline in the last two decades and not its success!

In the last 10 to 15 years, American multinationals have lost large parcels of strategic ground to Japanese and German companies. Why has this occurred, and why is it still occurring? Corporate America has never been as engrossed in techniques and formulas of competitive analysis and strategy as in the last 10 to 15 years. Yet America's competitive position worsens. Our work has convinced us that American executives are being "out-thunk" by their Japanese and German competitors. Our research clearly shows that brain wins over brawn over the mid-to-long term.

While American executives get mesmerized by "recipes" that come out of American business schools and are developed by professors whose research has been conducted in the business school library—with little relationship to business world realities—foreign competitors not entranced by these approaches are "eating their lunch."

The worst offenders of the last two decades have been the following techniques developed by the following people:

- The Portfolio Matrix techniques, which were based largely on the PIMS studies that came out of Harvard Business School
- The Competitive Advantage techniques also developed by a Harvard Business School professor
- The Shareholder Value techniques developed at Northwestern University

All of these approaches are conceptually flawed.

The Portfolio Matrix Approach—Marketing Mania!

The Portfolio Matrix approach, developed by the Boston Consulting Group and based largely on the PIMS research, contends that the two most significant factors to success are market share and market growth. By placing these two variables on horizontal and vertical axes, a matrix was developed that cataloged different business units into "dogs," "cash cows," "stars," and so on. The approach relied on the concept that to be the most profitable, a corporation had to have the largest market share.

Companies invested heavily in programs to increase their market shares, only to find themselves, in some instances, with the largest share of their markets, yet the least profitable among their competitors. Moreover, a number of companies with minuscule shares, but very clear business strategies, were sometimes found to be the most profitable. A good example is General Motors and Daimler-Benz: Although GM has the largest worldwide market share and Mercedes the smallest, Daimler-Benz has consistently outperformed GM in terms of profit.

After 10 years of widespread use during the 1970s, the market share/market growth approach to strategy was abandoned because of its destructive analysis of a business based on only two variables.

Competitive Analysis: Going Forward... Backwards!

Competitive analysis concepts, were, in our view, to the 1980s what the Portfolio Matrix formula was to the planning results of the 1970s. The thrust of competitive analysis is based on the underlying assumption that corporate strategy *starts* with an analysis of competitive position. That is a very myopic view of strategy. Furthermore, a strategy developed entirely on competitive analysis will always be, by its very nature, a *reactive* strategy and not a proactive one. And that is why most American businesses have been in a reactive mode for the last 15 years.

Akio Morita, founder of Sony, certainly did not have any competitive data in mind when the decision to introduce the VCR or the Walkman was made. None existed. In fact, strategy based on competitive analysis may only make the organization overlook other lucrative opportunities outside its *existing* competitive arena. If Sony had limited its strategy to looking only at its competitors in the transistor radio arena, its first product, it would never have developed the VCR or the Walkman. Obviously, a much broader strategy, based on factors other than its current competitors, was at work in Mr. Morita's mind.

Competitive Theory Is Myopic

The gurus that espouse competitive strategy as the tool to manage an organization successfully, in our opinion, are taking a very myopic view of business and the reasons why a business succeeds or fails. These gurus usually subscribe to the "value-chain" concept. This concept suggests that you compare your "system" of bringing your product to its intended user to that of your competitors. The suggestion is then made that if you wish to remain competitive, you should be looking for ways to "add value" into as many steps of the chain (thus "value-chain") as possible. There obviously is some rationale to this concept. However, adding value to each component of your chain may never give you a competitive advantage, or it may give you a temporary advantage that may quickly disappear. This might happen because you may be trying to add value randomly to the wrong parts of your business or to areas that competitors can quickly duplicate. In other words, you might not be adding value or competitive advantage to areas that are of strategic importance to you. As a result, you will always be in a reactive mode and not be in control of the "sandbox."

The way to control or influence the sandbox is not to deal with a competitor by trying to come up with better competitive tactics on a product-by-product or market-by-market basis, but by managing the overall *business strategy* of that competitor. Another important observation we made while working with CEOs running successful organizations was that many don't think that having or not having competitors would greatly alter the success or failure of their strategy. They believe that *their* own actions, and not those of a competitor, are the cause of their success or failure.

In our judgment, the "competitive" gurus fail to recognize two important elements of strategy:

1. Competitive activity is only *one* element of strategic analysis and not the exclusive one.
2. There is a major difference between *business strategy* and *competitive tactics.*

Our suggestion is that the development of a strategy for a business requires a different process than that of competitive analysis and should be done *before* any attempt to develop competitive tactics. Your competitors may not be the ones you think they are!

Over the last 15 years, we have worked with the chief executives of some 300 corporations worldwide, both large and small, trying to codify the thought process that a CEO and the management team use to formulate a coherent and successful strategy. That work has shown us, over and over, that competition is indeed a variable in the strategic process but that it *is not* the first variable to consider, nor is it the most important. During our work with CEOs, competition was almost never their major preoccupation. In fact, most of them were more concerned with competitors they did not yet have than with current competitors.

Who's the Competition?

Another difficulty in trying to develop a strategy by starting with an analysis of the competition is trying to determine who the competitors are. Competition *used* to be United versus American Airlines, each offering the same regulated fares. Or Macy's versus Gimbels. Or Ford and Chevy. Or Coke and Pepsi. Today, competition is exacerbated by technology, government intervention or lack of intervention, lifestyles, perceptions, growth, changing industry structure, new knowledge, demographics, and a host of other variables. United and American now compete in an unregulated environment against other low-cost carriers in a time when many buying decisions are made on the basis of frequent-flyer bonus points. Gimbels is gone, and Macy's competes with everything from other large chains, to K-mart and Bloomingdale's, to small boutiques offering personalized service, to the local drugstore right down the block which has become a mini-department store. Competition, because of change, is becoming more difficult to identify, harder to anticipate, harder to track, harder to understand, and much harder to combat. Competition no longer encompasses your traditional competitors. It now includes anything—anyone, any organization, any movement—that takes your customers' money away from you. So movie theaters now compete with home video rental centers and cable TV; the post office now competes with Federal Express, and both compete with electronic mail; your bank competes with Merrill Lynch and Sears Roebuck, all of them offering a variety of competing financial services; Greyhound and Trailways buses now compete with *airlines*, of all things, offering no-frills fares, and both compete with Amtrak; board games compete with video games and computer games; mail-order catalogs compete with computer shopping; travel agents compete with direct, desktop computer reservations systems.

Trying to determine who one's competitors are is sometimes akin to trying to find out "Who's on First?" As the CEO of a major company told us, "Our major competitor is also our major supplier as well as our most important customer." Today, one has to view competition in terms of alternative ways for the consumer to obtain the *results* desired, not as specific companies within your industry trying to underprice or outperform you. While the latter competition will always exist, it is just one component of the overall competitive picture.

The competitive analaysis approach to strategy is beginning to show signs of its limitations and is starting to unravel as the magic recipe of forward planning. In a recent article in *Business Month,* R. T. Pascale had this to say about that approach:

> So you think you've got a winning formula. You can diagram it. It fits on the grid. It worked well last year. Wonderful. Until you finally realize you missed the business opportunity of a lifetime.
>
> You've all heard about this "value-chain," those company activities that can be diagrammed and locked up in grids to point out the supposed source of competitive advantage.
>
> United Parcel Service, has been squeezing the maximum out of its value-chain as a parcel-delivery service. But by concentrating narrowly on how parcels should be moved (mostly by truck) and at what speed (three to five days), UPS missed the burgeoning market for faster, one-day air delivery that was pioneered and exploited by Federal Express. UPS is still trying to catch up.

Here's another example of the limitations of the Competitive Analysis approach: In the mid-1980s, the CEO of a billion-dollar communications company called on the business professor who originated this concept to develop a strategy to bolster its sagging performance. At this time, the company was divided into three divisions. The business professor called for a massive restructuring of the organization into 21 "market focus" segments. The intent was to enable disparate parts of the organization to create synergy by pooling resources and capitalizing on new, computerized electronic delivery systems.

Senior management praised the plan and predicted that the reorganization would double corporate revenues in just six years. In fact, results were disappointing, to say the least. The reorganization caused massive internal disruptions. Hundreds of jobs were sacrificed. Instead of creating synergy, the fragmentation of business units into "market focus" groups in most instances eroded whatever synergy had been present.

During the six years after the reorganization, company revenues, far from doubling, grew less than 5 percent and the company forfeited its long-time leadership position in a key industry segment. Ironically, the divisions that performed best over the six-year period were those that underwent the least amount of restructuring. The tale comes full circle. Ten years after the restructuring, the company reorganized again—back into three divisions, organized along functional lines.

It's easy to be seduced by the tidy theories of high-powered academic gurus—especially for the beleaguered CEOs under pressure to improve corporate performance. This Competitive Analysis approach is a very myopic view of business strategy. It is one element of corporate strategy, but not the *only* one. Sound strategic thinking accompanied by a structured process can broaden management's peripheral vision and help them develop a proactive and, eventually, more successful strategy.

Shareholder Value-Based Planning Is Strategic Folly!

The latest quantitative game in town is "shareholder value." This system encourages CEOs to judge businesses on their ability to enhance or reduce value for the shareholders. It also encourages CEOs to trade businesses on this criteria alone. This is strategic folly. Figure 1-1 depicts business's strategic choices.

The logic is simple. What may be in the best interests of the shareholders may not be in the best interests of the business. For example, getting rid of a business unit that is unprofitable may seem to be in the best interests of the shareholders. However, that

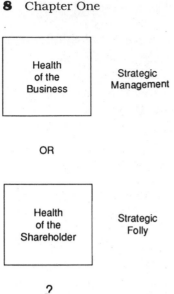

OR

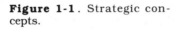

?

Figure 1-1. Strategic concepts.

business unit may be the proprietor of a key technology that is at the root of every one of the other, more profitable divisions.

Our view is that the most important criteria management should use to make strategic decisions is that of first enhancing the *health of the business*. If this is done consistently, the health of the shareholder will follow. A good example is Johnson & Johnson.

Johnson & Johnson has been one of America's best managed companies for several decades. And its priorities are clear to every member of the management team. These are well articulated in the J&J Credo:

- J&J's first responsibility is to our customers.
- J&J's second responsibility is to our employees.
- J&J's third responsibility is to our community.
- J&J's last responsibility is to our shareholders.

This hierarchy of strategic criteria has been in place since General Johnson formulated them in the 1920s; these criteria were in use when this author worked there in the 1960s, and they are still the guiding principles for the nutcracking decisions that J&J management make today. Witness their experience with Tylenol and the poisoned capsule problem they had in Chicago. Although the Chicago police told J&J management not to withdraw the product because the problem was only being seen in the Chicago area and that batch had been shipped nationwide, it was a no-brainer for J&J management to make. The health of the customer comes first. The product was withdrawn from every shelf in the world—a $350 million decision that obviously was not in the best interests of the shareholders in the short term but in the best long-term interests of the business. Had the hierarchy of priorities been reversed, I suspect the decision would have been much different.

When Gerber faced a similar problem—some glass particles started appearing in their baby food jars—management decided not to withdraw the product in an attempt to please the shareholders rather than their customers, only to find out later that they pleased neither. Their customers left them in droves, and their profits plummeted as did the value of Gerber shares.

The same principles that guide J&J exist also at Merck. They were articulated in 1950 by the founder's son, George Merck, and repeated in the 1990 annual report: "We try never to forget that medicine is for people. It is not for profits. The profits follow, and if we have remembered that, they never fail to appear." Merck's stock performance over the last several years would confirm this approach.

Phillip Kotler of the Kellogg School of Business at Northwestern University noted in his book *Marketing Management* that "[t]oo many US corporate leaders focused their attention on the stock market and not enough on the real market...they pursued profits first and customer satisfaction second."

William Copulsky of Baruch College points out that in a study he conducted, most companies that place shareholder value first usually do not do as well for their shareholders as those companies that dedicate their existence to the best interest of their customers. He goes on to illustrate why this occurs:

- Use of short-term strategies to boost the stock price
- Use of creative accounting to show higher earnings

- Cost cuts, which result in lost business because service, research, facilities, and goodwill deteriorate

Copulsky also notes in his article "Balancing the Needs of Customers and Shareholders" (*Journal of Business Strategy,* Nov./Dec. 1991) that "a quick scan of last year's corporate reports indicates that companies likely to stress shareholder value are companies with decreases in earnings. Those with a favorable record of stock appreciation are less likely to mention it; shareholders know when their share value is being increased."

Our own experience confirms this conclusion. In fact, our view is that the companies producing the best value for their shareholders over the long term are those that manage to a clear strategic focus geared to some principle that encourages management to manage in the best interests of the business first. The remaining chapters in this book explore how successful CEOs formulate and articulate such a concept.

A good example of a CEO who follows this approach is William Fife of Giddings & Lewis, the machine toolmaker. When Fife arrived in 1987, he found a company struggling financially. But, as *Forbes* reported in 1991, "...he knew that intelligent reinvestment, not slavish cost-cutting, is the key to a company's long-term commercial health."

Fife aggressively reinvested in his company's future. Expenses for research and development hit 10 percent of sales in 1990, compared with an average of 3 percent for U.S. industry as a whole.

The results? Since 1987, the company's sales have doubled from $125 to $242 million, and earnings have reached $1.85 per share—all this while U.S. industry overall is in a tailspin and Giddings' major competitors have not grown during the same period. In fact, some—the Japanese in particular—would argue that the corporation exists first and foremost for the benefit of its employees, a point of view difficult to challenge in view of its success over the last 30 years.

Malcolm Currie, ex-CEO of Hughes Aircraft, put it best when he stated: "Complex systems get into trouble when your approach is 'ready...fire...aim'" (*Fortune,* January 27, 1992).

2
Coping
with Change

If Charlie Chaplin were alive today, it would please him to remind us that his view of a changing world in his film *Modern Times* is as valid today as it was 60 years ago. In fact, many of the trends he explored in his classic movies are still with us, only they are happening more quickly. Change, obviously, has always been an integral part of business life. Some organizations, however, seem to cope with change better than others. In the future, the ability to handle change successfully will become even more vital. As we see it, several major areas of change will have a profound effect on business in the future, and the executives who will be able to lead their organizations through these changes will be the ones to survive and prosper.

Global Markets, Multiple Cultures

The first type of change that is accelerating is globalization. Although this phenomenon has been discussed in numerous books and articles, there are some characteristics of globalization

Portions of this chapter have been excerpted from the author's two previous publications, *The Strategist CEO* (copyright 1988 by Michel Robert) and *The Essence of Leadership* (copyright 1991 by Michel Robert). Both books are published by Quorum Books, an imprint of Greenwood Publishing Group, Inc., Westport, Conn.

that are not always understood. First, barriers to trade are coming down all over the world; Europe has set 1992 as a target date to finally become a common market. The United States and Europe are exerting great pressure on Japan to open its borders and are starting to succeed. I am convinced that not a single person could have predicted the extent or the rapidity of the changes that occurred in 1989 across eastern Europe or, for that matter, those that are currently taking place in the former Soviet Republics, which along with China, will become more important trading partners of the West. The consequence is that companies can no longer plan without considering the world as their marketplace. The recent fight for Firestone by Bridgestone of Japan, Pirrelli of Italy, and Michelin of France is a good example. The fact that the automobile market has become global is forcing tire manufacturers themselves to become international competitors. Cummins Engine Company, which dominated the U.S. market for many years, suddenly found itself surrounded by new competitors in the 1980s. The competition first came from Europe—Volvo and Mercedes-Benz—and then from the Japanese manufacturers Komatsu and Hino.

Even a very successful midsize client of ours in the Northeast, which has carved out a very comfortable niche for itself in the chemical industry, suddenly found one morning that a new Japanese competitor was establishing a plant only a few hundred yards up the road.

The consequence of the internationalization of business is the impact it will have on corporate planning. Decisions affecting product design, manufacturing sites, marketing approaches, distribution systems, and customer service will vary greatly from one market to another. The reason is simple. Although the marketplace will be global in scope, it is not now, nor will it be, homogeneous in character. In Europe, language and culture differ in each country. Customs and traditions vary greatly from one Asian nation to the next. Even the United States is becoming multicultural with the advent of immigration by Hispanics, Koreans, Japanese, Filipinos, and Vietnamese, to name but a few groups that are changing the fabric of the United States more than during any immigration wave of the past.

Sir John Harvey-Jones, former chairman of Imperial Chemical

Industries (ICI), explained the phenomenon well, as stated in *The Wall Street Journal*, at a meeting of the American Chamber of Commerce in London. "The cliche that the world is a single market is, in reality, not true. Each market requires different responses and it is the ability to read that response and apply that response which will be the key." This will require companies to be global in perspective but culturally sensitive on a market-to-market basis. Gary DiCamillo of Black & Decker told *The Journal of Business Strategy* (Nov./Dec. 1989) how his company is trying to cope with this phenomenon.

> As you go around the world, many power tools are used in similar ways so that there need not be major differences in the products...We don't need to reinvent the power tool in every country, but rather, we have a common product and adapt it to individual markets. The products are marketed quite differently in some cases due to local customs.

Think Global, Act Local

Historically, U.S. companies have not been very adept at operating across geographic or cultural boundaries. Japanese, Dutch, West German, and Swedish companies have shown greater versatility in dealing with a multicultural business world. Sony, for example, made a different Walkman for Norway than it did for Sweden, even though these countries were two of its smallest markets. American executives have not traveled or lived abroad as much as executives from many other countries. Japan's companies were sending hundreds of thousands of their executives to study and live in the United States in order to master English, U.S. customs, and American culture several years before they set about to conquer U.S. markets.

One of our long-term clients, 3M, has been a rare exception to the U.S. experience. At 3M there is a slogan that permeates all the foreign subsidiaries: "Think global, act local." This will be a fundamental rule of success in the future. Companies will have to act locally in a marketing and selling sense in order to flush out the distinctive needs of each market, and globally on a manufacturing, distribution, and customer service basis in order to achieve the required levels of critical mass for costs and value.

The need for executives to become "global strategists: working as deftly in Tokyo as in Toledo," as *U.S. News & World Report* (March 7, 1988) suggested, will accelerate in the twenty-first century. American business will have to learn global strategies and tactics in order to compete successfully. Overseas corporations are more skillful at developing strategies for foreign markets because they have been doing business outside their own countries for decades and can better navigate in unfamiliar terrain. U.S. business is not being assisted by U.S. business schools which, for the most part, teach techniques based on concepts that apply primarily to the domestic market and, therefore, are parochial and outdated in today's global marketplace.

More Competitors and More Intense Competition

The next trend that will become accentuated in the twenty-first century will be that of competition. As barriers to competition go down, more and more companies will see the world as their market and will want to jump into the game. The U.S. auto market used to belong to the "Big Three"—General Motors, Ford, and Chrysler. With the coming of Toyota, Nissan, Honda, and Subaru, that is no longer true. Hyundai, from Korea, has also entered the game. One must remember, however, that there are 12 car manufacturers in Japan, and Malaysia has just set up a car assembly plant. Each of these manufacturers will have to play the global marketplace in order to survive in its domestic market. This will bring not only more competitors but also more severe competition. Corporate executives will require finely tuned competitive skills in order to prosper into the twenty-first century.

The same trend is occurring in the financial markets. With the advent of the "big bang" day in London in the summer of 1987, the world of financial service companies has not been the same. Financial service companies that had never heard of each other suddenly became bitter rivals. The playing field has also changed dramatically in the health-care and airline industries because of deregulation. Deregulation, which started in the United States, is a policy that is beginning to spread abroad, with Europe now considering it.

Scarcer Human Resources

Employees will be a scarce resource for American companies in the next century. One reason is a result of the downsizing U.S. companies did in the 1980s. Downsizing may have made these organizations "lean and mean," but early retirement programs have deprived them of valuable experience and talent. Fewer, and younger, people are now required to make more important decisions than they ever had to before.

Furthermore, the current phenomenon of the "aging of America," whereby it is forecast that 50 percent of the population will be older than 55 by the year 2000, will result in an insufficient pool of younger people to replace the retirees. Corporations will have to find ways to substantially improve productivity without the benefit of experience. The Japanese have already solved the first problem; Japan's automobile industry produces the same number of cars as its U.S. counterpart, but with 700,000 fewer people.

Some skills will be in short supply. Engineers, in particular, will be a sought-after group. The number of engineers being graduated from U.S. schools is far less than in Japan and Germany, and also far less than what America requires.

Better Quality

The Japanese started the trend for better quality. By bringing in Dr. Deming and Dr. Juran to teach their work force better techniques of quality control and thus improve the performance and reliability of their products, the Japanese have now made quality improvements the standard operating procedure worldwide. And because of the enormous strides made by the Japanese and seen by consumers around the world, quality is again perceived as a desirable element for which consumers are willing to pay. Unfortunately, the Germans and the Japanese lead the world in quality; and it will take years for the United States, which is far behind and trying to catch up, to obtain even marginal improvement. Almost a decade after having caught the "quality" bug, U.S. car manufacturers have shown a 25 to 40 percent improvement in quality. However, U.S. cars still have 88.6 defects per 100 cars versus 47.3 defects per 100 cars for the Japanese. This gap will take years, if not decades, to close.

Most U.S. companies that were faced with the "Japanese challenge" in the 1970s reacted in the wrong way. They accused the Japanese of exploiting cheap labor and gaining market share by underpricing U.S. companies with lower priced, "me-too" products. Unfortunately, that was not the case. One company, when presented with the "Japanese challenge," saw it differently. Cummins Engine, in a February 1988 *Management Review* article, explained, "In our view, share gain by the competition [Japanese] was mostly won fair and square, with better products, better quality, better prices, and better responsiveness to the customer."

Instead of crying to the government for protection against Japanese firms, Cummins set about to help itself by redoubling its efforts in three areas: product price, cost, and performance. Cummins also taught its employees to remove the word *foreign* before *competition* and replace it with the word *international*. This took the emotion out of the issue and encouraged people to address rationally the problem of potential loss of market share. As a result, Cummins has not lost a single point of its domestic market share (in fact it has gained market share), and it has increased its international sales dramatically.

GM, Ford, and Chrysler have not found a way to sell their cars in Japan, yet the Japanese cannot get enough Volkswagens, Mercedes, Volvos, and BMWs. The difference, in our opinion, derives from the same reason why these products attract U.S. customers—better quality.

Information Explosion

Another trend that will exacerbate industry challenges in the next decades is the increase in the amount of information to which executives will have access when making decisions. IBM estimates that with the advent of personal computers (PCs), supercomputers, and on-line databases, managers will have seven to ten times more information available to make decisions in the year 2000 than they have today. There is no doubt that more accurate information contributes to better decision making. It is also true,that too much information can paralyze decision making. Waiting for more, or perfect, information can delay a decision and cause the decision maker to "miss the boat." In the twenty-first century, people will require more acute skills and thinking processes to be able to differentiate between relevant and irrelevant information more quickly and thus make better and more timely decisions. There will also be less room for error because most wrong decisions will have greater and more far-reaching negative consequences. A minor decision gone wrong may have repercussions around the globe.

Quantitative versus Qualitative Planning

The foundation of most corporate planning systems in place today is internally generated data—highly *quantitative* and historical in nature. Most long-range planning systems look back at five years of history—the numbers—and extrapolate for the next five years. This kind of planning does nothing to change the "look" or the composition of a business in terms of products, markets, and customers. It also assumes that outside influences will remain the same, in terms of competition, government, labor, and resource availability.

Most strategic planning systems we see in place in corporate America today are operational, or long-range, in nature. As such, they fail to take the whole picture into account. These systems are usually accompanied by a need to do a lot of analysis, usually requiring graphs, forms, bar charts, matrixes, and volumes of numbers.

Numbers Planning Discourages Risk Taking

An article in *The Academy of Management Executive* (February 1988, vol. 11, no. 1) brings home the idea that numbers planning discourages risk taking quite clearly. The authors Charles Hill, Michael Hitt, and Robert Hoskisson point out that, compared to other countries such as Japan, Germany, Italy, and even the United Kingdom, America's declining competitiveness over the last five years is owing to a decrease in both *product* and *process innovation.* They attribute this decline to the "quantitative" management systems espoused in the United States, such as "ROI-based financial controls and portfolio management concepts." These principles, they argue, "give rise to a short-term orientation and risk avoidance."

> The argument to this point has been that reliance on tight financial controls by the corporate office encourages decision-making at the divisional level consistent with short-run profit maximization and risk avoidance. The result is lower innovative activity and declining competitiveness.
>
> Many market losses experienced by American firms can be attributed to a *lack of emphasis* on *product* and *process innovation. Product innovations* create new market opportunities, and in many industries are the driving force behind growth and profitability. *Process innovations* enable firms to produce existing products more efficiently. As such, process innovations are one of the main determinants of productivity growth. In this technologically dynamic era, without a continual stream of product and process innovations, firms soon lose their ability to compete effectively.

The "risk avoidance" style of management in existence today in many U.S. companies has already cost America dearly. Many inventions, born in America, have seen the light of day as innovative new products abroad. One example is the transistor, invented by Bell Laboratories but exploited by Sony of Japan. A second is the videocassette, invented by California-based Ampex but exploited by Sony and JVC.

Strategic Planning
Discourages Innovation

The numbers approach of strategic planning can kill innovation. Even when employees come up with a good new product concept, management does not always have the nerve to pursue it.

Another signal of this trend is seen in the number of patents issued in the last few years. For 25 straight years—until 1986—General Electric, the powerhouse of American innovation, was the leader in terms of the number of patents issued to a company. In 1990, General Electric tumbled to fifth place (and to eighth place in 1991), surpassed by four Japanese companies: Hitachi, Toshiba, Canon, and Mitsubishi Electric. The Japanese registered over 18,000 patents in 1990, an increase of 25 percent over 1986. Canon has had a remarkable record, pushing its annual number of patents from 158 to 868. During the same time, General Electric's went from 822 to 785 patents. Even the Germans and the French are increasing their patent registration by 15 and 19 percent, respectively, while the United States' share is decreasing. The trend, unfortunately, is increasing each year. From 1980 to 1990, the percentage of patents granted to American corporations has declined from 62 to 53 percent.

3M has a standard by which it measures the performance of all its business units: 25 percent of each unit's sales must come from products that did not exist five years before. This criterion has caused 3M to introduce some 200 new products each year and has earned 3M a reputation as one of America's most innovative companies. Unfortunately, the same cannot be said for most industries in the United States.

Over the last few years, we have had the opportunity to work with many fast-growing midsized companies run by their original founders, and we have noted that these companies know only too well that continuous profits are best generated by a steady stream of new products. Because of the numbers focus, however, we see a growing need for better strategic management of large corporations. A management approach based more on the assessment of the qualitative variables facing the business, together with a need to rejuvenate the innovative juices for corporate America, is sorely needed.

Strategic Thinking versus Strategic Planning

Most organizations we have worked with have very elaborate strategic *planning* systems in place. Strategic planning, however, does not strategic *thinking* make! In fact, in many organizations, strategic planning systems are the death knell of strategic thinking. Most strategic planning systems we have seen are nothing more than systems that force people to make extrapolations of historical numbers. They oblige managers to look back at five years of history and make numerical projections for the next five years by adjusting for costs, inflation, share, and so on. This type of planning does nothing to change the direction, or composition, of the company. It's "straight-ahead" type of planning. In many organizations this annual exercise becomes a fire drill that everyone does by rote and that no one gives much thought to. These five-year projections are then catalogued in a large book, the book is then placed on the credenza, and nobody looks at the projections until the same time the following year. In fact, if someone did look at them, he or she probably would find that the numbers were nowhere close to what really happened.

In an article entitled "How to Prepare for 1995," *Fortune* (December 31, 1990) stated:

> At too many companies strategic planning has become overly bureaucratic, absurdly quantitative, and largely irrelevant. In executive suites across America, countless five-year plans, updated annually and solemnly clad in three ring binders, are gathering dust—their impossible specific prognostications about costs, process, and market share long forgotten. Asks John Walter, CEO of R. R. Donnelley & Sons, America's largest printer: "Do I have the books in my closet with all the numbers in them? Yes. Do I look at them? No."

Strategic Planning: The Death Knell of Strategic Thinking

Organizations that embarked on time-consuming planning systems imposed them on management, insisting that these "strategic plans" be addressed every 12 months. Because of the "fire drill" orientation of strategic planning systems, strategic thinking in many major organizations came to a standstill. *There simply wasn't time to think strategically.*

America's obsession with the "fire, ready, aim!" syndrome led to America's decline during the 1970s and 1980s. Even Michael Porter, in an interview in *The Economist* two years ago, admitted that "strategic planning in most companies has not contributed to strategic thinking. The need for strategic thinking has never been greater." The irony of this statement is that Porter's own techniques have been contributing to the erosion of strategic thinking.

If the preceding techniques are not conducive to setting strategy, what is then and how does a CEO go about developing and implementing a successful strategy?

The process needed to determine the future direction of an organization is not strategic planning but, rather, *strategic thinking.* Strategic thinking is a process that enables the management team to sit together and think through the qualitative aspects of its business and the environment it faces. The team can then decide on a *common* and *shared* vision and a strategy for the future of its company.

Unfortunately, most firms we work with have been so involved with the numbers approach to strategic planning that, in many of these organizations, *thinking strategically* has virtually disappeared. America will regain its competitive edge when organizations scrap these quantitative approaches to planning and institute the process of encouraging strategic thinking instead.

"The phrase gaining currency" states *Fortune* magazine in an article entitled "How to Prepare for 1995," "is *strategic thinking.*" Unfortunately, *Fortune* did not go on to describe what strategic thinking is. But we shall. The remainder of this book is intended to give you an in-depth understanding of the key concepts and process of strategic thinking.

3

The CEO's Vision: The Starting Point of Strategic Thinking

"My job," says Ken Olsen of Digital Equipment Corporation in a 1986 *Business Week* article, "is to make certain that we've got a strategy and everybody understands it." This statement is probably the best job description for a CEO we have come across. However, it's easier said than done!

Our firm has been involved in the area of strategy since the mid-1970s. Back then there was an explosion of literature on the subject of strategy, and we started browsing through these books to try to get an understanding of what strategy meant. Unfortunately, we became more confused than enlightened. The reason was simple. Each person who wrote about strategy used the word with a different meaning. Some authors said that *strategy* was the goal or objective; and *tactics* were the means. Others gave the word *strategy* a completely different meaning; they said that the *objective* was the goal and that *strategy* was the means. These two definitions are 180 degrees apart.

Another characteristic we noticed about these books was that most of them were written by professors sitting in business school libraries who had never even talked to the companies about which they were writing. In fact, their formulas were developed by trying to recreate the "magic recipe" that such-and-such company had followed to become successful. Our approach was different. We said to ourselves, "Let's go out and talk to people who actually run organizations. Let's find out what *strategy* means to them!" And that is precisely what we did. We went out and started interviewing CEOs in a variety of industries and in different sizes of companies. Eventually, we even participated in the sessions these CEOs had with their key people while they were wrestling with the issue of strategy. We were present, in the "war room," in hundreds of companies while managements were attempting to cope with the issue of business strategy and direction. What you will find in this book are the concepts and key ideas that we saw discussed and debated. The process described in the remainder of this book is a reflection of the thought patterns we saw effective CEOs use.

The first observation we made, while sitting in on these sessions, was that the people who ran a company had a "vision" (Figure 3-1) in their head as to what they wanted that company to "look" like at some point in the future. Most of these CEOs' time was then spent articulating, communicating, and explaining that

Figure 3-1. The vision of strategic thinking. (*Copyright © 1989 by Decision Processes International. All rights reserved.*)

vision to everyone in the organization. That vision became the magnet of everyone's activities and efforts.

Fortune magazine (September 23, 1991) referred to Sam Walton, the founder of Wal-Mart, in the following terms: "No one in the history of business could possibly have pursued a vision with more single-minded focus than has Sam Walton, which is why— in the twilight of life—he's still at it."

Daniel Ferguson, CEO of Newell Company, also has a vision. In an interview with *Forbes*, Ferguson explained that he "sees the business as a place to apply his original vision: Producing disposable products for mass consumption at the lowest manufacturing and distribution costs. He expects that as more and more people work at home, retail sales of office supplies will climb."

Even the CEO of Samsung, the Korean giant, is guiding his company following his vision of making Samsung a leader in machinery, telecommunications, computers, and chemicals. To demonstrate the extent to which this vision drives the decision making of that company, Samsung has installed 2000 phone lines free of charge in the Russian city of St. Petersburg in return for a $1.2 billion contract to overhaul its phone system.

Naturally, other people only embrace a CEO's vision if they understand it and agree with it. The vision, therefore, must be based on sound rationale—thus, the need for a process we call *strategic thinking,* the objective of which is to assist the CEO formulate and articulate this vision to key executives in order to get successful implementation. Moreover, strategic thinking is a process that also involves the management team because people will better implement something that they have helped to construct rather than something that has been imposed on them.

Our work and experience with CEOs have shown that most CEOs have great difficulty articulating and communicating their vision. As a result, they are not always successful in getting their people to implement it. Roger Smith, the ex-CEO of General Motors, may have said it best in a 1989 *Fortune* article just prior to his retirement.

> If I had an opportunity to do everything over again...I sure wish I'd done a better job of communicating with GM people. I'd do that differently a second time around and make sure they understood and shared my vision for the company. Then

they would have known why I was tearing the place up, taking out whole divisions, changing our whole production structure. If people understand the *why*, they'll work at it. Like I say, I never got that across.

In most organizations, the vision is implicit and resides in the head of the CEO. People around the CEO end up having to guess what the vision and strategy are. Unfortunately, their guess may be wrong as often as it is right. As a result, decisions are made—some of which tug the organization to the right, some to the left—and the organization zigzags its way forward.

George Schaefer, ex-CEO of Caterpillar and one of our clients, came to the same conclusion: "An explicit strategy is absolutely essential. Implicit is not good enough in the competitive environment in which we operate today." George Bush had a similar dilemma during his 1988 campaign for the U.S. presidency when he was faulted for his inability to articulate his vision for America. It became and is still referred to as "the vision thing" problem.

Extracting and rendering explicit the vision of the CEO is not an easy task. It's not a question of simply asking the CEO, "Where are you taking this organization?" or "What do you want this company to become?" Our experience with these types of questions is that they elicit answers that are numeric in nature; most CEOs would reply: "We will be a billion dollar company," or "We will have the largest market share," or "We will be the most profitable in the industry." These are *not* statements of vision. They are statements of the *results* of a vision. The vision must be stated in terms that determine the "look" or composition of the company at some point in the future. In order to describe what the organization will "look" like in the future, one must go through a process we call strategic thinking.

No Process for Thinking Strategically

When company executives finally recognize the need to do some strategic thinking, they often say, "Let's go up to the mountaintop for the weekend, away from these damn telephones, and let's spend a couple of days thinking about where this company is headed."

When they get to the mountain and lock themselves into a room, they put their elbows on the table, look at each other, and say, "Okay, where do we start?" Because they don't have a formal process to follow, within five minutes they're back to discussing operational issues, and the real future of the company is never addressed.

What sort of questions should company executives be asking themselves? In most organizations, there isn't a *process* for strategic thinking. Moreover, all the highly quantitative strategic planning methodologies, tools, and techniques popular during the last 10 years have almost brought thinking to a standstill because everybody has been exercising the wrist and resting the brain.

A viable strategic thinking process has to start with the organization's leaders, its top management. When they get together, instead of addressing operational issues, they should look at their future environment, talk about the organization's future direction; they should develop a strategy and articulate their "vision" or future profile for the company.

What Is Strategic Thinking?

Strategic planning, in our view, is not a replacement for sound *strategic thinking*. What, then, is strategic thinking?

Strategic thinking is the process of thought that goes on inside the head of the CEO and the key people around him or her that helps them determine the "look" of the organization at some point in the future (Figure 3-2). And that look, or composition, of the business in the future may be different than it is today. Strategic thinking can be compared to picture painting. It is the process that helps the CEO and the management team "draw a picture" or "profile" of what they want the organization to look like at some point in time. It is this "picture" or "profile" that will determine the direction, nature, and composition of the business. *Strategic thinking, then, is the type of thinking that goes on within the mind of the CEO, the strategist, to shape and clarify the organization's future strategic profile* (Figure 3-3). Decisions that "fit" within the parameters of this profile are taken and implemented, and decisions that do not "fit" the profile are rejected.

Copyright 1988 Decision Processes International
All Rights Reserved.

Figure 3-2. The process of strategic thinking. (*Copyright © 1989 by Decision Processes International. All rights reserved.*)

Figure 3-3. Strategic thinking profile. (*Copyright © 1982 by Decision Processes International. All rights reserved. Revised 1990.*)

Strategic thinking is different from both *strategic planning* and *operational planning*. In fact, strategic thinking is the *framework* for the strategic and operational plans (Figure 3-4).

Strategic thinking can also be described as the type of thinking that attempts to determine *what* the organization should look like. In other words—the *strategy*. Operational planning, and even what has become known as strategic planning, is the type of thinking that helps us choose *how* to get there. To illustrate the

Figure 3-4. Strategic thinking framework.

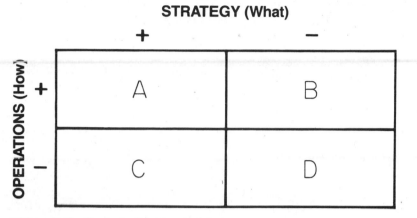

Figure 3-5. Strategic thinking matrix.

difference between the two types of thinking, we can develop the matrix in Figure 3-5 with the *what* on the horizontal axis and the *how* on the vertical axis. We can complete the matrix by further dividing each axis into *good* (+) strategic thinking and *poor* (-) strategic thinking as well as good (+) operational or strategic planning and poor (-) operational or strategic planning. Although both of these activities go on in all organizations, what we have noticed is that they go on with various degrees of proficiency

In quadrant A (Figure 3-6), we find companies that do both very well. They have developed a *clear profile* and explicit strategy, and they manage their business successfully on an ongoing

Figure 3-6. The A quadrant.

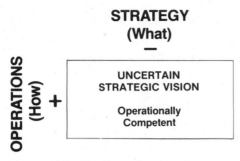

Figure 3-7. The B quadrant.

basis. Companies that fall into this quadrant are IBM, Sony, Daimler-Benz, Harrod's, Johnson & Johnson, Honda, Boeing, and Procter & Gamble.

In quadrant B (Figure 3-7) we find companies that have been successful by managing their ongoing operations effectively, but which cannot articulate *where* they're going. Generally speaking, many of the companies in the United States have been in this quadrant since the early 1970s.

In quadrant C (Figure 3-8) we find the opposite situation. Here are companies that have a very clear strategy, but management has difficulty implementing it operationally. During the 1980s, one such group of companies were the manufacturers of PCs. Each company probably had a very clear strategy—"be the best IBM clone we can be." However, many of these companies had

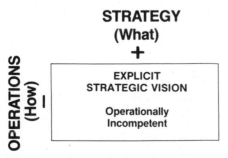

Figure 3-8. The C quadrant.

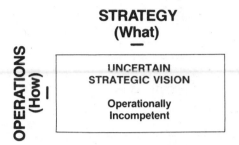

**STRATEGY
(What)
—**

**OPERATIONS
(How)**

UNCERTAIN
STRATEGIC VISION

Operationally
Incompetent

Figure 3-9. The D quadrant.

great difficulties making this strategy occur; thus, their fortunes went up and down like yo-yos.

The last quadrant (Figure 3-9) is the worst of both worlds. Here we find organizations that do operational and strategic planning poorly. Companies that fall into quadrant D usually don't survive very long, so it is difficult to generate a long list. But two companies currently attempting to come out of this quadrant are Chrysler and AT&T. For many years, Chrysler has not known whether it should compete with Ford and General Motors at one end of the spectrum or with Toyota, Nissan, and Honda at the other end. Although Chrysler has attempted to drastically improve its operational effectiveness in the 1980s, we doubt that its strategy and eventual profile is any clearer than it was before.

Which quadrant is your organization in (see Figure 3-10)?

Although we would all like to say that we are in the A (+/+) quadrant, most of our clients readily agree that they fall in the B (-/+) one. That is—they are effective operationally but aren't always sure what direction they are pursuing. As a matter of fact, our experience has shown that almost 70 to 80 percent of companies are in that position.

Companies falling in quadrant B can be referred to as being part of the Christopher Columbus School of Management.

- When he left, he didn't know where he was going.
- When he got there, he didn't know where he was.
- When he got back, he couldn't tell where he had been!

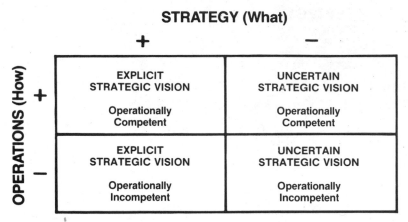

Figure 3-10. Strategic thinking matrix—completed.

But he got there and back three times in seven years! Which means that Columbus was operationally very competent although he never knew where he was.

The strategic thinking *process,* therefore, can be described as the type of thinking that attempts to determine *what* an organization should "look" like in the future. *Strategic planning* systems, on the other hand, help choose *how* to get there.

Strategic thinking is a fresh approach to the subject of strategy. It identifies the key factors that dictate the direction of an organization and is a *process* that the organization's management uses to set direction and articulate their vision. For strategic thinking to be successful, it is necessary to obtain the commitment of the organization's key executives and the commitment of others who will be called upon to implement that vision. Naturally, the vision is greatly shaped by the CEO.

It's a process that extracts from the minds of people who run the business their best thinking about what is happening in the business, what is happening outside in the environment, and what should be the position of the business in view of those highly *qualitative* variables (opinions, judgments, and even feelings)—not the *quantitative* ones. Strategic thinking produces a vision, a profile, of *what* an organization wants to become, which then helps managers make vital choices. It enables management to put the corporation in a position of survival and prosperity within a changing environment.

What Is the Content of a Strategic Vision?

If one were to draw a "picture" of the future look of a company (Figure 3-11), what would the picture contain? A very good question! And one we asked ourselves. Another way to ask the same question could be: "How does the `look' of the company translate itself into physical evidence?"

In other words, if someone asked me to invest a million dollars in his or her company on the basis that it would be a "good bet," I would certainly ask myself:

Where is this company going?

What will it "look" like down the road?

The answers would help me to determine, in advance, if it will be a good bet!

Therefore, I would start looking for physical indicators of that company's direction and its eventual look. The things that would serve as physical indicators of the company's strategy, direction, and eventual look include

- Its product catalogue (current and announced)

Figure 3-11. The vision as a "strategic profile."

- Its people and the skills management are trying to draw to the organization
- The markets it serves
- Its competitors
- Its customers
- Its suppliers
- Its market segments
- Its R&D budget
- Its facilities

In fact, there are numerous things I could look at for this company, or any other—each of which would serve me as an indicator of the direction and eventual "look" of that company. However, from that long list, four items are the true reflection of a company's strategy, direction, and eventual look (Figure 3-12).

- The nature of its products
- The nature of its customers
- The nature of its market segments
- The nature of its geographic markets

Everything else that goes on in an organization is either an input to these or an output from these four items. Capital, people,

Figure 3-12. The principal areas that reflect a company's vision and profile.

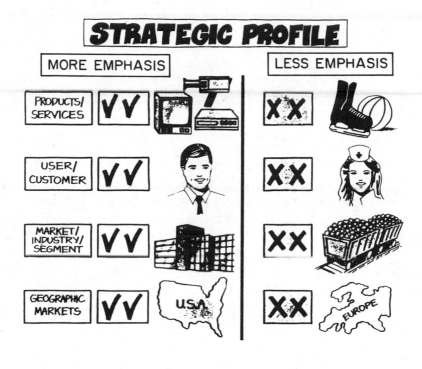

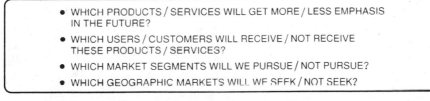

Figure 3-13. (*Copyright © 1982 by Decision Processes International. All rights reserved. Revised 1990.*)

skills, facilities, and technology are all inputs. Profit, earnings, and dividends are all outputs.

Thus, the most important questions (Figure 3-13) management must ask themselves and answer if they want to shape the look of their company over time are

- Which products do we offer? But more important, which products do we *not* offer?

- To which customer groups do we offer these products? But more important, to which customer groups do we *not* offer these products?
- Which market segments do we seek? But more important, which market segments do we *not* seek?
- Which geographic areas do we pursue? But more important, which geographic areas do we *not* pursue?

To us, it is more important for management to understand what the strategy *does not* lend itself to. Why is this so?

The management of a company conducts two activities that will go to alter the "look" of that company over time. First, every year through the budgeting process, management allocates resources. Unless they have agreed to a profile such as the one illustrated in Figure 3-13, it will be very difficult for them to allocate resources logically and strategically. Instead, the organization usually ends up in a tug-of-war over resources. This happens because each business unit manager promises more results if given more resources. If management takes away resources, however, each manager will then request a reduction of the results he or she will be asked to produce. Plans then get compared to each other and, usually, the most loquacious manager wins. Our view is that plans should not be compared to each other, but rather to the "vision" or "profile" of the future organization we are all trying to build. Actions and programs contributing to this vision obtain resources, and actions or programs not contributing to this vision do not. Thus the strategic profile becomes a *tool to allocate resources strategically.*

The second management activity that will alter the "look" of the company over time is deciding which opportunities to pursue and which ones not to pursue. There are always opportunities facing any organization, but, as we all know, some opportunities are much better than others. Therefore, management must have a tool, or filter, to discriminate between opportunities. Again, the strategic profile fills this void. Opportunities that have the characteristics of items designated to receive "more emphasis" in the future will be pursued, whereas those on the "less emphasis" list will not.

The result of a sound strategic thinking process must, in our view, produce a very clear profile of the kinds of products, customers, market segments, and geographic areas that the strategy of the business *lends* itself to and that *will* thus receive emphasis, but more important, the kinds of products, customers, market segments, and geographic areas that the strategy of the business *does not lend* itself to and, thus, *will not* receive emphasis in the future.

How does management go about determining where the line of demarcation is so that when an event occurs they can quickly judge whether or not it fits their strategy and vision? What is it that drives the strategy of a business and, thus, the decisions of management, for determining what to emphasize or de-emphasize? Chapter 4 will answer these questions.

4

Determining the Strategic Heartbeat of the Enterprise

What is it that determines the nature of the products, customers, market segments, and geographic areas that a company pursues and those that it does not? How does management decide which of these it seeks to pursue and not pursue? The answer to these vital questions is the most important element of thinking strategically. It is a concept we call *driving force* (Figure 4-1).

In order to explain this concept, one must look at an organization as a body in motion. Every organization has momentum, or motion. Every organization is going forward in *some* direction.

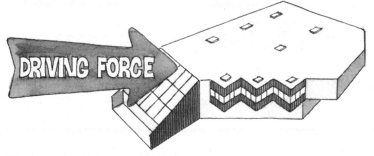

Figure 4-1. The driving force.

Our suggestion is that there is something pushing, propelling, or *driving* it in that direction. The concept of driving force or *strategic drive* is that one element or component of a business drives the organization toward certain products, markets, and customers and thus determines that organization's "look" or profile. The concept of driving force is synonymous with a similar idea from Shepherd's Laws of Economics, "Behind each corporation must be a singular force, or motive, that sets it apart from any other corporate structure and gives it its particular identity." It is the identification of what drives and gives an organization its momentum in a certain direction that is the key element of strategic thinking. It becomes imperative, therefore, for the top executives of a company to have a clear understanding of the concept of driving force if they wish to better manage or even change the direction of their organization.

One test of a company's strategy comes when management is assessing future opportunities. While working with the CEOs of many corporations, we observed that new opportunities were always put through a hierarchy of filters. The final filter always seemed to be the search for a "fit" between the opportunity and one key component of the business. Some CEOs looked for a fit between the products the opportunity brought and the organization's current products—Fiat's acquisition of Alpha Romeo is a good example. Others looked for a fit in the similarity of its customer base or the markets served. Still others looked for a fit of technology. Some companies looked for a fit to its selling method. If a close fit was found, then the opportunity was considered. However, if the relationship was not seen as a close enough fit, then the opportunity was abandoned.

The search for an area of strategic fit varied from one company to another. But it was always the same one in each company. In other words, *one* element of the organization was driving its business strategy. The more successful the company, the more the CEO recognized that the organization's strategy was anchored around a key component of its business. It is this *strategic area* that is the heart of a company's business and what gives it an edge in the marketplace.

What are some of the key components of a company that drive the strategy of the business, and thus, the decisions of management as to what they choose to emphasize or de-emphasize?

Every organization, we found, is composed of ten important strategic areas:

- Product/service concept
- User/customer class
- Market type/category
- Production capacity/capability
- Technology/know-how
- Sales/marketing method
- Distribution method
- Natural resources
- Size/growth
- Return/profit

Although all ten of these components are present in most organizations, only one of these is *strategically* most important to a company and is the engine that propels, or drives, the company forward to success. Unfortunately, in many companies, the key area that gives a company its strategic edge is not always understood by management itself. Once a company's management understands which driving force is at the root of the company's strategy, decisions about the types of products, markets, and users that will bring competitive advantage are made more successfully.

Depending on which of these ten strategic areas is most important to a given organization, the decisions it makes about future products, users, and markets will vary greatly. Because each of these strategies can lead the organization in a different direction and greatly alter its future profile, management must choose which *one* it will pursue in order to gain competitive advantage. To illustrate the effect of each strategy, we offer the following definitions.

The Concept of Driving Force and/or Strategic Drive
Product/Service Concept–Driven Strategy

A product concept–driven company is one that has "tied" its business to a singular product. As a result, this company's future products will greatly resemble its current and past products in "look" and "function." Future products will be modifications, adaptations, or extensions of current products; that is, derivatives of existing products. In these companies, there is a "genetic" linear relationship among past, present, and future products.

The automobile industry is a good example. The "look" and "function" of an automobile have not changed for one hundred years and probably will not change for the next one hundred. Thus, General Motors', Daimler-Benz's, and Volvo's business concepts represent product-driven strategies. Boeing also follows this type of strategy. Its business is built around the concept of an airplane, and the next product from that company will probably be another "flying machine." IBM is yet another company that is product concept–driven—the "product" being computers and various derivatives, including mainframes, minis, micros, PCs, and laptops.

User/Customer Class–Driven Strategy

A user/customer class–driven company is one that has deliberately anchored its entire business around a describable and specific category of end users or customers. The company then tries to satisfy a range of related needs that stem from that class of end user. And it responds with a wide variety of unrelated products that are always aimed at the same group of end users/customers.

Playboy, for instance, is a good example of a company pursuing a user class–driven strategy. The phrase "entertainment for men" on its magazine cover spells it out quite clearly. As such, Playboy is into magazines, hotels, casinos, cable television, video cassettes, calendars, and so on. These are all genetically unrelated products that are managed in very different ways. What they have in common is that they are geared to the young, single, affluent male.

Johnson & Johnson, whose strategy of making products for "doctors, nurses, patients, and mothers" is another such company whose entire business strategy is driven by the health-related needs of these four categories of people. All of J&J's products—from Band-Aids to sutures to shampoo to talcum powder—are all genetically unrelated, but they are all aimed at these four classes of individuals. J&J could easily tweak its Band-

Aid technology to make electrical tape for example, but it would never do that since the buyers of electrical tape are electricians—not a class of users that J&J wants to serve.

Market Type/Category–Driven Strategy

A market type/category–driven company is similar to the user/customer class–driven company except that, instead of having its business limited to a set of end users, the market type–driven company has anchored its future to a describable market category.

An example is American Hospital Supply. The company's name identifies the *market* to which its business is anchored—the hospital. The strategy of the company is to respond to a variety of needs coming from that market. As a result, the product scope of such a company ranges from bedpans to sutures to gauze pads to electronic inaging systems and whatever else a hospital might need.

Production Capacity/Capability–Driven Strategy

The company that is production capacity/capability–driven usually has a substantial investment in its production facility, and the strategy is to "keep it running" or "keep it full." Therefore, such a company will pursue any product, customer, or market that can optimize whatever the production facility can handle. Paper mills, hotels, and airlines are good examples of capacity-driven organizations. Keeping the facility at full capacity is the key to profits. Print shops are another class of business pursuing this strategy. A printer will tend to accept any job that the presses can handle, and optimizing the use of those presses leads to profit.

Technology/Know-How–Driven Strategy

A company that is technology/know-how–driven is one that has the ability to invent or acquire hard or soft (know-how) technology. Then it goes out looking for applications of that technology or know-how. Over time such a company gets involved in a broad array of products, all of which stem from the technolog, and serve a broad array of customers and market segments.

This organization uses technology to gain competitive advantage. It fosters the ability to develop or acquire hard technology (e.g., chemistry) or soft technology (know-how), and then looks for applications for that technology. When an application is found, the organization develops products and infuses into these products a portion of its technology, which brings differentiation to the product. While exploiting this edge in a particular market segment, the company also looks for other applications in other segments. Technology-driven companies often are "solutions looking for problems" and usually create brand new markets for their products. "The funny thing about this business," says CEO Edson de Castro of Data General in a *USA Today* article, "is that things are designed and brought out when no market exists"—a syndrome that a technology-driven company frequently encounters. "It's always been technology that has driven this company," de Castro adds. 3M, Sony, Du Pont, and Polaroid are other examples of technology-driven companies. Du Pont's invention of nylon led it to market segments as diverse as nylon stockings, nylon carpets, nylon shoes, nylon thread, nylon sweaters, nylon fishing line, nylon tires, and nylon-laminated packaging materials. The only link between all these diverse businesses is that they all stem from one technology—nylon.

Sales/Marketing Method–Driven Strategy

A sales/marketing method–driven company has a *unique* way of getting an order from its customer. All products or services offered *must* make use of this selling technique. The company does not entertain products that cannot be sold through its sales method, nor will it solicit customers that cannot be reached through this selling or marketing method. Door-to-door direct selling companies such as Avon, Mary Kay, Amway, and Tupperware are good examples. Other examples are catalogue sales companies and the Home Shopping Network. Whatever HSN can demonstrate on a TV screen, it will entertain as part of its strategy.

The direction of these companies and the products and markets they pursue is determined by the selling method. Amway or Tupperware would never operate in an area where door-to-door selling is prohibited. Their decisions regarding future products are also determined by their selling method. Whatever their salespeople can place in their carrying bags will determine the nature of the product these companies promote.

Distribution Method–Driven Strategy

Companies that have a *unique* way of getting their product or service from their place to their customer's place are pursuing a distribution method–driven strategy. Telephone operating companies, with their network of wires from their switches to the outlets in the walls of your home or office, are an example. A telephone company will only entertain products or services that use or optimize its unique distribution system. Food wholesalers are another example. Department stores such as Sears are a third. Sears' jump into real estate and financial services is an attempt to optimize the use of the company's distribution system. Karl Eller, ex-chairman of Circle K convenience stores, had a very clear understanding of his company's driving force: "We're a massive *distribution system.* Whatever we can push through that store, we will" (*Forbes,* November 3, 1986). Wal-Mart, Supervalue, and J. C. Penney are others.

Natural Resource–Driven Strategy

When access to or pursuit of natural resources is the key to a company's survival, then that company is natural resource–driven. Oil and mining companies are classic examples.

Size/Growth–Driven Strategy

Companies that are interested in growth for growth's sake or for economies of scale are usually pursuing a strategy of size/growth. All decisions are made to increase size or growth. LTV and Gulf & Western in the 1960s and 1970s were examples of companies following this strategy. Peter Grace's "philosophy of size and diversification, often at the expense of earnings" makes W. R. Grace & Company another example.

Return/Profit–Driven Strategy

Whenever a company's only criterion for entering a marketplace or offering a product is profit, then that company is return/ profit–driven. Conglomerates are usually good examples. They are often organized along the lines of a corporate control body with fully autonomous subsidiaries. There are usually few or no links between these subsidiaries except a certain level of profit. Subsidiaries are bought or sold on this criterion alone. ITT, under Harold Geneen, had such a strategy. His dictum of *an increase in quarterly earnings, regardless what* and the subsequent acquisition of some 275 unrelated businesses, showed strategic disregard for all other criteria.

The Strategic Heartbeat of the Enterprise Determines What Kind of Company You Become

One of 3M's largest businesses is its tape division. When 3M first developed masking tape and all of its other derivatives, it discovered an enormous market, to the point that this division is still considered to be a "crown jewel" to this day. My friends at 3M told me that soon after the discovery of this product, there was a heated debate among 3M executives as to whether 3M should stay focused on this single product or whether it should diversify into other arenas. One group claimed that 3M was a "masking tape" company, a product concept–driven strategy, and should not deviate from this product and market. Another group claimed that 3M was a polymer chemistry–based company, a technology-based strategy, and should explore other applications for that know-how. Luckily for 3M, the latter group won and 3M went on to find numerous other successful applications for its polymer chemistry expertise in the form of other products such as audio tape, video tape, diskettes all the way to Post-it™ Notes. Had the product concept–driven strategy group won, 3M would be a substantially different, and smaller company today.

Another example is B. F. Goodrich. Once a dominant player in the tire business, the company viewed itself as a tire company—a product concept–driven strategy. Because of its inability to compete in this business in the 1970s, the company sold off its tire business and redefined itself. Luckily, the CEO, John Eng, decided that Goodrich was not a product-driven business but rather a technology-driven one based, again, on its knowledge of chemistry. The company had a long history of chemical innovation going back to the 1920s when it first developed PVC, one of the world's most used plastics. Eng decided to bring the company back to its roots and today Goodrich is into a broad array of chemical applications from cosmetics to pharmaceuticals and is a much healthier company.

Because of the downsizing of the defense budget in the United States, another company that is trying to redefine itself is the maker of the B-2 bomber, Northrup. Traditionally a maker of airplanes, a product-driven strategy, Northrup now finds itself facing a bleak future and is looking to diversify into new markets. Luckily, its CEO, Kent Kresa, knows what the company's heartbeat is. "We understand lightweight, strong structures that travel at high speeds," he says. "That's our technology." With this technology-based strategy in mind, as opposed to its former product-driven one, Northrup can continue to make aircraft, possibly even commercial ones, but at the same time it can explore opportunities outside this crowded arena, such as rail and mass transit equipment.

Understanding the strategic heartbeat (driving force) of the enterprise is, to us, fundamental to determining the opportunities that the enterprise should explore which eventually will shape the "look" or profile of the corporation.

Strategic Questions

Some key *strategic* questions for the CEO and each member of the management team at this point are:

- What is your *current driving force?*
- What should your *future driving force* be?
- What impact will your driving force have on your products, markets, and customers?

The answers we have received from the management teams of client organizations have been varied and frequently surprising, even to these executives themselves.

Questions Often Asked about the Concept of Strategic Drive

In strategy sessions with the top management of many companies in North America, Asia, and Europe, several interesting questions have been asked when discussing the notion of what is driving their strategy.

Are There Not Multiple Driving Forces Present Simultaneously in a Company? I call this the "Sybil" syndrome. Sybil was, as the movie of the same name depicted, a woman with multiple personalities who had great difficulty living with herself. The same is true in business. A company cannot be something one instant and something different the next. Each company, like all individuals, has a unique personality that is based on one element of the business that dominates over the other elements of that business when nutcracking decisions are made about allocation of resources or choice of opportunities.

In a single product, single market, single customer–base company, that single driving force is clear and permeates the entire company. It is in a multiple product, multiple customer, multiple market–type company that we see the blurring of driving forces and accompanying business concepts (Figure 4-2).

In these types of companies one finds a hierarchy of driving forces and accompanying business concepts being practiced simultaneously. However, it becomes important for management to understand what this hierarchy is because some configurations can coexist well while other configurations are inherently incompatible. Take, for instance the case of a company whose corporate driving force might be that of a certain *technology* while one of its divisions might wish to pursue a *user class*–driven strategy. These

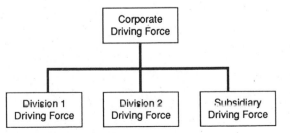

Figure 4-2. Corporate driving force.

two strategies are inherently incompatible. The corporate body is saying that it wants all its divisions to pursue opportunities around applications of its unique technology regardless of customer segments, but the division is pursuing a strategy anchored to a restricted class of end users with products that do not necessarily stem from the corporation's key technology. No degree of management skill will ever resolve this inherent strategic incompatibility.

It is important to know what the *driving forces/business concepts* are in order to:

1. Ensure that the divisional strategies are compatible with the parent's.
2. Prevent any overlaps between the division's strategies.

Is Not, Then, Profit the Only Strategic Driving Force for a Company? This is a legitimate question because one cannot survive in business without profit. However, unless the company is a financial conglomerate à la ITT, the driving force is usually not profit. Profit is the *result* of one's strategy, not its objective. The analogy I use to explain this conclusion is that of eating. In life, one must eat to live. That's a given. If one does not eat at least once or twice a day, one will die—guaranteed! The same is true in business. Every business must be profitable to survive, that is a given of business life, otherwise the company dies. But surely the purpose of life is not eating! There must be another purpose to life, although one must eat each day to live. The same is true in business. Surely, there is a purpose to a company other than that of making a profit, although it must produce a profit in order to survive. Profit is the *result* of strategy, not its objective. Profit tells one how well or how badly the strategy is working, but usually there is another purpose behind the existence of each company. In other words, some other driving force is at the root of the company's existence.

If It Is Not Profit, Then Should Every Company Be Customer-Driven? *Every organization must be customer-sensitive.* The rationale of this statement is that if your products do not fill certain user needs, the products will not succeed. Every organization, regardless of which driving force propels it, must make products that satisfy the needs of its customers. However, that alone does not make the company user class–driven. In other words, every corporation must be *user-sensitive,* but not all corporations are *user class–driven.*

Depending on which driving force it is pursuing, each organization is user-sensitive, but in a different manner. Here are some examples:

- *Product concept–driven.* This organization is user-sensitive in that its people are looking for new users of its current products, or else it is looking to satisfy new needs within its current user group with slightly modified products.
- *User class–driven.* This organization is user-sensitive in that its people are in a continuous dialogue, usually with a well-known or captive user, to try to identify the user's unique new needs that can be satisfied by totally new or different products.
- *Technology-driven.* This organization is user-sensitive in that its people are looking for users that have applications for a technology which the organization has or is willing to acquire. Once applications are found, then products are designed and developed.
- *Production capability/capacity–driven.* This organization is user-sensitive in that its people are looking for users who offer products or services with components that can be substituted, replaced, or supplemented with their own so that they can optimize the capacity of their production facility.
- *Sales/marketing method–driven.* This organization is user-sensitive in that its people are looking for new products/services that can be sold to existing users through its current selling method or new users that can be reached through the same selling method.
- *Distribution method–driven.* This organization is user-sensitive in that its people are looking for new products/services that can be sold to existing users or new users who can be reached through its current distribution system.

Is There Not a Natural Evolution from One Driving Force to Another Over Time for Any Company? Another very good question. Again, however, the answer is no. Furthermore, if you feel that the driving force of the company is constantly changing, you have a clear indication that the company is drifting. In other words, there is *no* strategy. A good strategy stays in place over a long period of time. Constancy of purpose is the key to strategic success.

Are There Not Some Legitimate Instances When One Wants to Deliberately Change the Strategic Drive of the Company? The answer, obviously, is yes. One such instance is when the current strategy runs out of growth. Growth is another given in business because every company needs growth to perpetuate itself. Therefore, when the strategy runs out of growth, management should deliberately seek to change the driving force and thus the strategy and direction of the company. One such example was the American Can Company some years ago. Its CEO, for reasons known only to himself, determined that the company was running out of growth and decided to radically alter its direction. Over a period of two to three years, all can and packaging operations were sold, and the funds were invested into the purchase of a number of financially oriented companies. The firm was renamed Primamerica and is today a financial services company.

Another example is Playboy Enterprises. Playboy's strategy of "entertainment for men," particularly young, single men is not growing any more because the absolute number of men that fit Playboy's profile are diminishing. As a result, Playboy has been struggling and looking for another strategy.

A second legitimate instance when management should rethink the driving force of its strategy is when there is something so threatening on the horizon that such a threat might completely invalidate the existing strategy. A case in point is Exxon. In the mid-1970s, Exxon ventured into arenas outside its traditional business—namely, the purchase of Reliance Electric and several emerging office equipment companies. My view about these ventures is that Exxon, at that time, was deliberately looking to change its strategic direction. And with good reason. It saw its driving force—access to natural resources—threatened. One only needs to remember what many countries were doing with their oil reserves back then—nationalizing them! If I had been in the shoes of Exxon's CEO, I also would have come to the conclusion that if this trend continued around the world, there would be no Exxon down the road. Therefore, I would have embarked on a course to change the direction of Exxon away from its dependence on oil. However, finding a new strategy as successful as the one already in place might require a long time and several attempts. Why do I posture that these ventures were conscious attempts to change the direction of Exxon even though the company lost $600 million in Reliance and over $200 million in office equipment? The reason is simple. No one was fired! What usually happens to a division manager who loses $600 or $200 million. Right—not at Exxon. And for this reason, this author contends that those were deliberate decisions made because Exxon management felt its strategic heartbeat was threatened and it was consciously looking to replace it. What happened then in the 1980s? The answer, again, is simple. The governments that had nationalized their reserves found out that reserves underground are not worth very much unless one knows how to bring them above ground. And who do you think does that best? Exxon. With the threat gone, Exxon in the mid-1980s rededicated itself to its first love—oil and gas—and sold off its nonstrategic ventures.

A third instance when the driving force of a company changes is when it changes by accident and not by design. This occurs more often than not in companies because management gets seduced by opportunities!

Seduced by Opportunities

The best time to detect whether or not a CEO has a strategy is to observe the management team at work when trying to evaluate opportunities, especially those somewhat remote from the current business. On these occasions we noticed that, when faced with unfamiliar opportunities, management would put these through a hierarchy of different filters. The ultimate filter was always a "fit" between the products, customers, and markets that the opportunity brought and one key element, or driving force, of the business. This is a clear signal that management had a sound filter for their decision. In other instances when there was no such filter in place, management would only look at the "numbers" and, if these looked reasonable, would jump aboard only to find out later that the opportunity had something else at the root of its business, which was its driving force, and gradually the opportunity would start pulling the entire company off course.

We also found that seduction is at its highest when the current strategy is producing more cash than the business requires. Such has been the case with Daimler-Benz in recent years. After pursuing the strategy of making the "best engineered car" for over one hundred years and making money every single year, Mercedes found itself in the mid-1980s sitting on a hoard of cash—$10 billion—which it did not need to run the business. It was at this point that the finance person recommended the purchase of a number of companies in totally unrelated fields. Over the objections of the CEO (who later resigned), but with the approval of the major shareholder (the Deutsche Bank), the company made a series of acquisitions from household appliances to airplanes. As could have been predicted, Daimler-Benz is currently struggling for the first time in its long history. Worse still, while the management of Daimler-Benz are preoccupied with these unfamiliar businesses, BMW is making significant inroads at its expense and has displaced Mercedes as the top selling car in Germany—its home market!

Another current example is Toyota. This company has been so successful in the last 20 years that it is now sitting on top of $25 billion that it does not need to finance its various businesses. So what is Toyota management looking to do with that money? Management is investigating the possibility of entering the aviation business, and Toyota thinks that it can exploit its engine and manufacturing capabilities, in which it excels, to this new business. My own view is that airplanes are a long way from being "genetically" related to automobiles and that Toyota will struggle in this new business and might even suffer in the car business while it is attempting this unfamiliar road. Good news for General Motors, finally!

The lesson? Beware of seduction. Management skills are not always easily transferable from one business to another. In fact, each driving force brings with it the requirement to develop a different set of key skills.

The essence of strategic thinking, therefore, is the CEO's and management's clear understanding of which component of the business is more important than all others and is the "heartbeat" of the business—and, as such, lends itself more to certain products, customers, market segments, and geographic markets.

5

Determining the Strategic Capabilities of the Business

As we observed companies over the years, we noted that there were some that could perpetuate their strategy successfully over long periods of time, like IBM or Daimler-Benz. Others, however, had great difficulty doing that, and their performance over time was akin to a yo-yo. What, we asked, made for the difference?

Over time, the strategy of an organization, like a person, can become stronger and healthier or it can get weaker and sicker. In our opinion, what determines which way the strategy will go are the *areas of excellence* that a company *deliberately cultivates* over time to keep the strategy strong and healthy and give it an edge in the marketplace. An area of excellence, another key concept of strategic thinking, is a *describable skill, competence, or capability* that a company cultivates to a level of proficiency greater than anything else it does and particularly better than any competitor does. It is excellence in these two or three key areas that keeps the strategy alive and working. Bill Marriott, of the hotel chain, stated, in a February 1988 article in *Fortune* magazine, that "it took the company over a decade to figure out that it had special expertise in running hospitality and food-service operations...." This "special expertise" or capability is what we call an area of excellence.

The deliberate cultivation of strategically important capabilities, usually two or three of them, keeps an organization's strategy strong and healthy and gives it an edge over its competitors. Losing these two or three skills weakens the strategy and eliminates the organization's competitive edge. Depending on which of the 10 driving forces is being pursued, the areas of excellence required to succeed will greatly change.

Keeping the Strategy Strong and Healthy

Product/Service Concept–Driven Strategy

A product/service–driven company survives on the *quality* of its product or service. Witness the automobile wars. Who's winning? The Japanese. Why are Americans buying Japanese cars and even willing to pay premium prices for them during this period of quota restrictions? The answer is simple: The Japanese make better cars. The bottom line for a product-driven strategy is: Best product wins!

One area of excellence is *product and process development*. Compared to American cars, Japanese cars of the late 1950s (when cars from Japan came onto the market) were far inferior. But Japanese car manufacturers understood well that pursuing a product-driven strategy required product and process development. And they strove to improve the product—to make it better and better—to the extent that Japanese cars eventually surpassed the quality of American cars.

For many years Amdahl and Data General were satisfied with making copycat versions of IBM mainframes. Both had mediocre performances. In 1991, however, both companies decided to stop matching IBM and to start making better computers than IBM. It's too early to tell, but this strategy is bound to produce better results.

A second area of excellence is *service*. IBM, which also pursues a product-driven strategy, is well aware of this requirement. Ask IBM clients what they admire most about IBM, and 99 out of 100 will say its service capability. IBM deliberately invests more resources in its service function than any other competitor and thus has a considerable edge in response time and infrequency of product failures.

In a product-driven mode, you maintain your competitive advantage by cultivating excellence in product development and service.

Market/User Class–Driven Strategy

An organization that is market/user class–driven must also cultivate excellence to optimize its strategy, but in dramatically different areas. A market/user class–driven company has placed its destiny in the hands of a type of market or a class of users. Therefore, to survive and prosper, it must know its user class or market category better than any competitor. *Market or user research*, then, is one area of excellence. The company must know everything there is to know about its market or user in order to quickly detect any changes in habits, demographics, attitudes, or tastes. Procter & Gamble, which is consumer-driven, interviews consumers (particularly homemakers), over two million times per year in an attempt to anticipate trends that can be converted into product opportunities. *Playboy* does the same thing by monitoring changes in its subscribers through its magazine surveys each year.

A second area of excellence for a market/user class–driven company is *user loyalty*. Through a variety of means, these companies, over time, build customer loyalty to the company's products or brands. Then they trade on this loyalty. Over time, Johnson & Johnson has convinced its customers that its products are "safe." And it will not let anything infringe on the loyalty it has developed because of this guarantee. Whenever a Johnson & Johnson product might prove to be a hazard to a person's health, it is immediately removed from the market.

The Tylenol case in Chicago (discussed in Chapter 1) is a good example of how highly Johnson & Johnson values its users' loyalty. Even though "experts" predicted the death of Tylenol because they reasoned that Johnson & Johnson's recall was an admission of guilt, three months later Johnson & Johnson reintroduced the product, showed how the company had eliminated the possibility of tampering, demonstrated that the product was "safe" again, and traded on their users' loyalty to regain sales. Six months later Tylenol once more had the largest market share.

Production Capacity/Capability–Driven Strategy

When there is a glut of paper in the market, the first thing a paper company does is lower the price. Therefore, to survive during the period of low prices, one has to have the lowest costs of any competitor. To achieve this, an area of excellence required is *manufacturing or plant efficiency*. This is why paper companies are forever investing their profits in their mills—to make them more and more efficient. An industry that has lost sight of this notion is the steel industry in the United States and central Europe. By not improving their plants, they have lost business to the Italians and Japanese, who have done so. One notable exception in the United States is Allegheny Ludlum, which has done very well because it has the lowest costs of any steel mill, including the Japanese and Italian mills. As a result, Allegheny's revenues and profits have consistently improved. Its managers are unique in that they know the cost of each of perhaps thirty thousand coils of steel floating around the company's seven plants, at any given stage of production. "The thing that scares me now is that we know our true costs, but competitors don't," says CEO Richard Simmons in a *Fortune* magazine article. "How can they make logical pricing decisions?"

Another industry, textiles, has lost a lot of ground to off-shore competitors, but one exception stands out. Guilford Mills in Greensboro, North Carolina, is competing very successfully, and the reason is that its chief executive, Charles Hayes, knows that, as a production capacity–driven organization, his company must excel at optimizing manufacturing efficiency. "We can make fabric as cheaply as anyone in the world," he says in an article in *Forbes* magazine (January 26, 1987). "We take that basic commodity, nylon lingerie fabric, and enhance it. The more we can do to it in the manufacturing process, the more we can sell it for and the higher our margins." In order to do this Hayes spends heavily on new equipment—over $36 million over two years to gain the most automated knitting, dying, and fiber plants in the world.

A second area of excellence for the production capacity–driven strategy is *substitute marketing*. Capacity-driven companies excel at substituting what comes off their machines for other things. The paper people are trying to substitute paper for plastic; the plastic people are trying to substitute plastic for aluminum; concrete for steel. The same is true in the transportation industry where bus companies are trying to replace trains; train companies the airlines; and so forth.

Technology/Know-How–Driven Strategy

A company that is technology-driven uses technology as its edge. Thus, an area of excellence required to win under this strategy is *research*, either basic or applied. Sony, for example, spends 10 percent of its sales on research, which is 2 or 3 percent more than any competitor. Its motto, "research is the difference," is proof that the company's management recognizes the need to excel in this area.

By pushing the technology further than any competitor, new products and new markets will emerge. Technology-driven companies usually *create* markets rather than respond to needs, and usually follow their technology wherever it leads them. Merck & Company is a good example of a company whose CEO and chief strategist, Roy Vagelos, knows precisely what area of excellence must be fueled to deliver new products. Merck, at Vagelos' directive, pours hundreds of millions of dollars into research, as a technology-driven company should, and has come up with an ongoing stream of new products (12 in five years) in an industry that introduces a new drug about as often as an aircraft manufacturer introduces a new airplane. It has consistently spent a greater share of its revenues on research than the rest of the industry. In 1986, the amount was $460 million, and it was increased to $1 billion in 1991, which was 11 percent of sales—more than any competitor. Its research teams *excel* and are on the leading edge of science in biochemistry, neurology, immunology, and molecular biology. Few other drug companies can match the breadth and depth of expertise Merck has in these areas.

Another CEO who has realized the importance of research as an area of excellence for his company is Edmund Pratt, Jr., of Pfizer Inc. From 1981 through 1990, he spent 8 percent of sales on R&D. In 1990 alone, the amount was $602 million, or 14 percent of revenues. Pfizer is in the process of launching nine new drugs which could have a potential of over $2 billion in sales for the company. "We've got new drugs coming out our ears," says a pleased Pratt in a 1991 *Forbes* article.

Also in the pharmaceutical industry, there is yet another CEO who clearly understands the relationship between his company's driving force and its areas of excellence. This is Robert Bauman of Smith Kline Beecham in the United Kingdom. In a 1992 article appearing in the *Journal of Business Strategy,* Bauman articulated it in this manner: "The unifying theme of the company has always been a science based strategy [technology driving force]." As such, he allocated 80 percent of the firm's $800 million budget to six therapeutic areas of excellence. These are anti-infectives, biologicals, cardiovascular, central nervous system, gastrointestinal, and inflammation and tissue repair. Bauman expects that by 1996 the company will be generating 25 percent of its revenues from these strategic capabilities.

A second area of excellence for technology-driven companies is *applications marketing.* Technology-driven companies seem to have a knack for finding applications for their technology that call for highly differentiated products. For example, 3M used its coating technology to develop Post-it™ notepads and some 60,000 other products.

Sales/Marketing Method–Driven Strategy

The prosperity of a sales method–driven company depends on the reach and effectiveness of its selling method. As a result, the first area of excellence companies such as Avon and Mary Kay must cultivate is the ongoing *recruitment* of door-to-door salespeople. Mary Kay has had tremendous success in the last few years because it has been able to draw several hundred thousand women to sell its product. Avon's fortunes have suffered because its sales force has dropped considerably during that same period.

The second area of excellence needed to succeed with this strategy is improving the *effectiveness* of the selling method. Door-to-door companies are constantly training their salespeople in product knowledge, product demonstration, and selling skills. Growth and profits come from improving volume through the diversity and effectiveness of its sales methods.

Distribution Method–Driven Strategy

To win the war while pursuing distribution method–driven strategy, you must first of all have the *most effective* distribution method. As a result, you must offer products and services that use or enhance your distribution system. Second, you must always look for ways to optimize the *effectiveness,* either in cost or value, of that system. That is your edge. You should also look for any form of distribution that could bypass or make your distribution method obsolete.

Both Federal Express and Wal-Mart are good examples of distribution method–driven companies. They are constantly striving to improve the efficiency of their respective distribution systems—the heartbeat of their business. David Glass, CEO of Wal-Mart, has stated, "[O]ur distribution facilities are one of the keys to our success. If we do anything better than other folks, that's it" (*Forbes,* August 10, 1987). Knowing that, Glass spent $500 million in the last five years in a computer system that links the company to its suppliers in order to lower costs even further.

Fred Smith, CEO of Federal Express, also knows what the strategic heartbeat of his business is when he says, "The main difference between us and our competitors is that we have more capacity to track, trace and control items in the system" (*Journal of Business Strategy,* July/August 1988).

Natural Resource–Driven Strategy

Successful resource-driven companies excel at doing just that—*exploring* and finding the type of resources they are engaged in. Exxon considers itself to be the best at "exploring for oil and gas," and it does this better than any competitor. It was the recognition of this fact that led Exxon to drop its office equipment division. There's not much oil and gas to be found there; plus, that kind of venture requires excellence in areas Exxon does not possess.

John Bookout, CEO of Shell USA, is a good example of a strategist who understands his company's areas of excellence. Shell's particular expertise is "enhanced oil recovery in offshore waters deeper than 600 feet." In this area, Shell has few rivals, as he explained to *Forbes* magazine. In 1983, Shell drilled a project called Bullwinkle in the Gulf of Mexico at a depth of 1350 feet. Outsiders thought the project was too risky, particularly since Shell did not spread the risk by taking other partners in on the deal. "You can't believe how easy that decision was," he says. "It took us 30 minutes in the boardroom." The reason? Bookout was banking on Shell's area of excellence in deep water recovery.

Size/Growth or Return/Profit–Driven Strategy

Companies that choose either a size/growth–driven or a return/profit–driven strategy require excellence in financial management. One such area is *portfolio management.* This means proficiency at moving assets around in order to maximize the size/growth or return/profit of the entire organization.

A second area of excellence is *information systems.* These companies usually have a corporate "Big Brother" group that constantly monitors the performance of its various divisions, and, as soon as a problem is detected, an attempt to correct or expunge it is made. Harold Geneen had such a group at ITT.

Importance of Areas of Excellence

Why are areas of excellence an integral part of strategic thinking? No company has the resources to develop skills equally in all areas. Therefore, another strategic decision that management must wrestle with, once the driving force has been identified, is to clearly identify those two or three skills that are critical and to give those areas *preferential* resources. In good times, these areas receive additional resources; in bad times they are the last areas you cut. For example, 3M, which is a technology-driven company, had a chairman—Alan Jacobsen—who clearly recognized this concept. When Jacobsen took over as chief executive, he set about to improve 3M's profitability. He asked all his division heads to cut expenses by as much as 35 percent but he spared R&D expenditures. In fact, he *increased* R&D from 4.5 percent of sales to 6.6 percent. The reason: Research is a required area of excellence for a technology-driven company. Ever since then 3M has been on a roll spitting out 300 to 400 new products each year, and its stock has more than doubled in the last five years.

A company, therefore, has two additional key strategic decisions to make if it wishes to succeed. First, it must determine which strategic area will drive the business concept and thus the direction of the organization. Second, it must decide what areas of excellence or competence it must cultivate to keep that strategy healthy. These areas of excellence should receive preferential treatment—fueled with more resources in order to develop a level of proficiency greater than any competitor. Once resources are diverted elsewhere, proficiency diminishes and the company loses its edge vis-à-vis its competitors.

Too often organizations are distracted from what has made them successful. The most successful organizations are the ones where the leader and senior management clearly understand their business concept and fuel the key areas of excellence required for success with more resources each year than they give to other areas. They then pursue this business concept with total dedication and without allowing any competitor to attain the same level of excellence in those few key capabilities. As Benjamin Disraeli so clearly noted many decades ago, "The secret to success is constancy of purpose." And as the CEO of J. P. Morgan, one of the world's most successful banks, said about the firm he heads: "We aren't likely to deviate radically from the clear strategic path we have been on since the days of the first Morgan partners" (*Dun's Business Month*).

Sometimes, an area of excellence or strategic capability is one that has been cultivated over a long period of time. Pioneer, the Iowa corn seed king, dominates its rivals because it has deliberately cultivated the skill of gene juggling to a higher level of proficiency than any competitor. The company develops more than 20,000 hybrids per year, of which only five to ten make it to market. And it has been doing this for over 65 years. The result has been an increase in farmers' yields from 40 to 110 bushels an acre.

Knowing what strategic area drives your organization and the areas of excellence required to support that strategy is akin to understanding what the strategic weapon is that will give you a distinct and sustainable advantage in the marketplace. Our experience has clearly shown that any strategy can work, but that no company can pursue two strategies simultaneously. No organization has the resources to develop excellence in several areas concurrently.

Understanding the concepts of strategic drive or driving force and areas of excellence makes life for the CEO and the management team much easier in terms of the decisions they make about new products, markets, and customers that constitute the future profile of the organization.

6

Articulating the Business Concept of the Enterprise

"Every practice rests on theory, even if the practitioners are unaware of it." So says management guru Peter Drucker in his book *Innovation and Entrepreneurship: Practice and Principles.* Another expert on the subject, Alfred Sloan who was CEO of General Motors in the first half of this century, put it this way in his book *My Years with General Motors:*

> Every enterprise needs a concept of its industry. There is a logical way of doing business in accordance with the facts and circumstances of an industry, if you can figure it out. If there are different concepts among the enterprises involved, these concepts are likely to express competitive forces in their most vigorous and most decisive forms.

Yet a third guru, Henry Mitzberg, has also made a similar observation, as reported in a 1980 article in *Harvard Business Review:*

> Strategy is the organization's "conception" of how to deal with its environment for a while. If the organization wishes to have a creative, integrated strategy...it will rely on one individual to conceptualize its strategy, to synthesize a "vision" of how the organization will respond to its environment. A strat-

egy can be made explicit only when the vision is fully worked out, if it ever is. Often, of course, it is never felt to be fully worked out, hence the strategy is never made explicit and remains the private vision of the Chief Executive.

It is also our view that every organization originates and perpetuates itself around a key idea or *business concept*. In many organizations, however, that business concept is not always clear or well articulated. It usually resides in the mind of the leader— rather than being explicit and in hard copy so members of the organization get a "feeling" of the concept and the direction of the firm from the nature of the decisions that are accepted or rejected by the leader over a period of time. Most people who head organizations have great difficulty verbalizing their business concept to their colleagues, and it is reflected in the nature of their actions.

Meaningless Mission Statements

Over the last few years we have noticed a substantial increase in the number of corporations attempting to construct mission or vision statements (Figure 6-1) that articulate the organization's business concept. Unfortunately, their efforts are often fruitless because of the lack of a structured process to help them. As a result, they end up with statements that are so "motherhood" in tone that everyone can agree with, but that are useless as guides to help people make daily operational decisions. Over time the statement is quietly ignored.

The Need for a Concise Business Concept

Our view on the subject of mission statements is simple:

- In our mind the words *strategy, business concept, mission, mandate,* and *charter* are all synonymous.
- A good business or strategic concept should be not longer than a paragraph. There is no need to have pages and pages describing what the business is about. However, every word,

"OK, how about -- 'to get real big, keep everyone in the world happy, and have George Bush in for lunch next week'?"

Figure 6-1.

modifier, or qualifier must be carefully thought through because each moves the line of demarcation between the products, customers, and markets that will receive more emphasis and those that will receive less.

- It is our opinion that the ability of people to execute a CEO's strategy is inversely proportionate to the length of the statement.

Therefore, the statement must be precise and concise.

The driving force concept is a tool that allows management to identify which area of business is at the root of the company's products, customers, and markets and is strategically more important to that company than any other area. However, it is also a tool that allows management to articulate its concept of doing business in that mode. We now need to formulate a one-paragraph statement that explains "how" this driving force will propel the organization and dictate its behavior when choosing future products, markets, and customers. This statement will be the conceptual underpinning of the business. Depending on which driving force is chosen, the organization's business and/or strategic concept will be dramatically different.

Examples of Business/Strategic Concepts

The following are examples of business concepts that we have helped our client organizations to construct. For reasons of confidentiality, the names of the companies involved have been omitted. In each instance, the driving force and the strategic heartbeat appears in italics.

The first is from a product-driven company (computers):

> Our strategy is to provide and support industry standard, real-time *computer systems* for *time critical* applications that require high I/O throughout and fast, predictable interrupt responses. We will do this in high potential industry segments that we can dominate with added-value, differentiated, reliable products, services, and tools that are easily configurable and can be tailored to meet the specific needs of these applications. We will do this in geographic areas where we can achieve enough critical mass to justify adequate support.

The second is also from a product-driven company (magazines):

> We will publish a thought-provoking, sophisticated women's *business magazine* that provides strategies to enhance the achievements of successful women who are in the vanguard of the business community. These independent thinkers create markets, drive markets, mold thought, and set ideals for their generation. We publish a magazine that demonstrates respect for our reader by speaking eye-to-eye to her. We address a complement of women's life choices and/or life cycles that are journalistically unique and are presented in a stylish and authoritative way.

A third example comes out of the insurance industry:

Our strategy is to provide innovative *property and casualty insurance products* and related services of high volume/value and distributed through carefully selected independent brokers and/or other effective methods.

We will tailor our products to respond to the evolving needs (business, lifestyle, ethnic) of these customer segments and that can by timely and cost effective delivery/distribution systems on leading edge technology.

We will strive to dominate the niches we choose to enter.

The next three are examples of user class–driven companies:

Our strategy is to listen to *printers* in order to identify productivity and/or quality improvement needs in the pressroom. We will respond with auxiliary, control, and material handling products that are differentiated and provide superior and reliable performance. We will do this in strong, long-term potential industry segments worldwide.

Our strategy is to seek out the nutritional and related management needs of *dairy producers* interested in improving the yield and productivity of their milk production. These producers should be in high density (low population) geographic areas. We will respond with unique and/or highly differentiated products and/or services that contribute to the economic benefit of the producer and provide enough ROI to perpetuate the growth of the business.

We will seek out the educational, environmental, or play value needs of *preschool, primary,* and *intermediate age youngsters.* We will respond with *distinctive* products that have high standards for quality, product, and service which can be marketed to teachers/parents or children through a variety of distribution channels.

The next example is that of a market category–driven company:

We will serve the global *cardiovascular market* through medical professionals with differentiated single patient use devices for therapeutic and adjunctive diagnostic purposes. These will be based on appropriate technologies and our anticipation of patients' and professionals' needs, and provide the highest quality and service.

The following examples are from technology/know-how–driven businesses:

> Our strategy will be to proactively exploit our *systems, engineering, and software* know-how to address performance/efficiency needs of real-time, on-line complex applications. We will respond with customized, integrated systems and/or subsystems, together with related support products/services, that add value and are differentiated by innovative content. We will pursue selected market segments giving more emphasis to the civil and geographic areas that can be supported locally over the long term and that meet our growth and profit targets. We will use our *electromedicine* know-how to exploit opportunities in therapeutic and closely related diagnostic modalities to treat human musculoskeletal disorders. We will respond with conceptually advanced, innovative, and proprietary products developed internally and externally.
>
> Our strategy will be to exploit our unique *self-dispensing technological know-how* by such as pH control, pressure filling metering valves, sleeve gasket nitrogen filling, pressure filling of liquified gasses and powders, and aluminum crimping. We will look for high margin applications that can lead to the creation, design, and manufacture of differentiated or even proprietary products. We will seek out applications in selected growth opportunities in diverse industrial markets worldwide based primarily on the following core technologies:
>
> - *Fluorochemicals*
> - *Specialty film*
>
> The products developed should have specialized functional properties with high perceived value and be proprietary in nature.
>
> Our strategy will be to seek and exploit applications for *digital signal acquisition,* processing, and presentation technologies and provide data analysis solutions that enhance the productivity of users. We will respond with high quality, differentiated products, services, and/or systems that bring added value and provide a substantial competitive advantage. We will do this primarily in selected worldwide nonconsumer market segments that can be serviced and supported.

The next example is from a production capability–driven company:

Our strategy is to innovatively exploit [our] unique mix of *steel forming, welding and coating capabilities* to market well-designed, low-tech, value-added components and products.

We will do this in geographic markets where these distinctive capabilities can provide a better competitive value package in design, price, quality, and/or delivery and primarily through distributors that add value in their right or directly to end users when appropriate.

The following one is from a sales/marketing method–driving force:

Our strategy is to use *direct-response marketing* methods to provide proprietary and primarily business-oriented products/services that satisfy perpetual, recognized or unrecognized needs and return healthy profits.

Another comes from a distribution method–driven company:

We protect and grow the *network business* (*local distribution and toll access*), by providing access, terminal products, and various support services to a wide spectrum of customers with varying communications needs.

Our final example is from a natural resource–driven business:

We will increase our asset value by maintaining a managed portfolio of risk/reward balanced exploration opportunities from which we will locate, define, and deliver *commercial deposits of oil and gas,* with supportive services, to our producing divisions.

The corporatewide mix of exploration projects will ensure the discovery of sufficient reserves form low-risk projects to provide a return that will exceed the cost of capital when burdened by the total corporate exploration costs including frontier projects and all other high-risk exploration projects. Any success from these high-risk opportunities will provide the upside potential for significant added value to our asset base.

Ideally, the business concept of the enterprise can be expressed clearly in a statement as simple as Wal-Mart's concept of "clustering scores of stores throughout a 200-mile area around the distribution points so that deliveries can be made every day." This distribution-driven concept is as uncomplicated as they come and is the heartbeat of that company and the root of its success.

Sometimes, however, the business is more complex, and, therefore, requires more detail and precision. Take, for example, this one from one of our clients:

> We will be among the leaders in the development and commercialization of selected *polymer bonded components and fiber reinforced composites.* The company will invest in, or acquire, businesses in strategically important product/market segments.
>
> We will produce specialty, engineered products and provide related services for heat resistant, inertia control, fastening, and lightweight structural component applications. The company will emphasize the use of its proprietary technology and manufacturing know-how to provide value-added, competitive products. These products will be produced and marketed worldwide for industrial, vehicular, aerospace, and military customers.

The "Bumper Sticker" Strategy

Even though we advocate a business concept no longer than a paragraph in length, many CEOs still find this too long and difficult to communicate. So many companies attempt to extract the essence of the statement and condense it down to "bumper sticker" size.

For example, our technology-driven client whose statement appears in the preceding section has captured the essence of its strategy in the phrase "Real-time systems for real world applications." In fact, this phrase has become the thrust of all of that company's advertising.

One CEO who clearly understands this concept is Steven Reinemund of Pizza Hut. "We're a *distribution* system for pizzas," he declares in a March 1991 *Fortune* article—thus his decision to extend Pizza Hut's stores in airports and malls.

Sometimes, the driving force will be found in the name of the company itself—Polaroid—obviously a technology-driven company whose business concept was founded on the Polaroid instant photography technology.

Even though different companies follow the same driving force, they may still have business concepts different enough from each other to be going down separate roads. Let's look at some examples in the automobile industry: Volvo, BMW, Mercedes, Volkswagen, and General Motors can all be said to be product-driven: automobiles and more automobiles. However, each of these companies has a very different conception of its product. For example:

Volvo—"safe and durable *cars*"

Mercedes—"best engineered *car*"

BMW—"the ultimate driving *machine*"

Volkswagen—"people's *car*"

General Motors—"a *car* for each income strata"

As a result, each of these companies goes down a different road and seldom competes with each other even though they all make cars.

Other examples of "bumper sticker" statements include:

- Federal Express's concept of "guaranteed overnight delivery of letters and small parcels"
- Koji Kobayashi's (ex-CEO of NEC) concept of the "convergence of computers and communications"—stated 30 years ago
- Thomas Watson's vision of "processing information," articulated over 50 years ago
- 3M's motto of "Innovation working for you"
- Sony's concept of the "ingenious use of electronic technology"

Each of the other categories of driving force brings with it a different business concept that can be more clearly articulated once the notion of strategic drive is understood.

The business concept influences all aspects of a corporation's activities. It determines the scope of products, customers, and markets; the organization structure; the technologies required; the type of production facilities; the distribution channels; the marketing and selling techniques; and even the type of people employed. Basically, it sets the tone, climate, and behavior of an organization.

It can also explain the behavior of the CEO. As Peter Drucker has stated in *Innovation and Entrepreneurship* about Thomas Watson: "Watson was an autocrat, of course. Visionaries usually are. Because visionaries cannot explain to the rest of us what they see, they have to depend on command."

It is imperative, in our view, that the business and/or strategic concept be explicit. Otherwise, it resides in the head of the CEO and people around him or her have to guess where the line is between activities that are acceptable within the strategy and those that are not. Unfortunately, they may guess wrong as often as they guess right. It is also our view that it is important for the CEO to involve the whole management team in the development of the business concept and the "bumper sticker." There are two reasons for this.

Lesson 1: People Don't Implement Properly What They Don't Understand!

One reason why the strategy may not be implemented properly is that it was developed by the CEO in isolation. Many CEOs have a strategy, but their key people are not involved in the process. In such a case, subordinates usually do not understand the rationale behind the strategy and will spend more time questioning it than implementing it. The CEO becomes more and more impatient as subordinates question his or her logic more and more deeply. The CEO, on the other hand, can't comprehend why people are not executing what, to the CEO, is a simple strategy.

Some CEOs might involve one or two people in the formulation of the strategy. This is better than doing it alone but is still not good enough. The *entire* management team must be involved in order to achieve accurate understanding and proper execution.

As Dale Lang, chairman of *Working Woman* and *McCall's* magazines, noted as a reason for using our strategic process, "I could have dictated to the staff what I wanted to do, but it's a whole lot better if they reach the conclusion themselves. In that way, they're working their plan and know how and why they chose it."

Lesson 2: People Don't Implement What They Are Not Committed To

Experience has shown that almost any strategy will work, unless it is completely invalidated by negative environmental factors. Experience has also shown, however, that *no* strategy will work if a couple or a few members of senior management are not committed to that strategy. In effect, if total commitment is not present, those uncommitted to the strategy will, on a day-to-day basis, do everything in their power to prove it wrong.

In order to obtain commitment, key managers must be involved at each step of the process so that their views are heard and discussed. Participation, although sometimes time-consuming, breeds commitment. Key managers buy into the strategy because they helped construct it. It is as much *their* strategy as the CEO's.

Many CEOs have used our process knowing in advance the outcome. They did so anyway, using it as a tool to tap the advice and knowledge of their people and to obtain commitment to the conclusion so that implementation of the strategy can then proceed expeditiously. The Japanese call this *nima washi*—bottom-up commitment.

7

Corporate or Business Unit Competition?

"Corporations don't compete, business units do." So says Michael Porter of the Harvard Business School in his book *Competitive Advantage*. This conclusion is based on the notion that as a company grows into an array of multiple products and customer groups, it ends up in a variety of different markets, each with a different group of competitors. Thus the need, and the Porter rationale, to separate the corporation into business units based on a product/customer matrix that places each unit "closer to the market" and increases its ability to compete successfully.

In our view, nothing could be further from the truth. Our own experience with all three hundred of our clients clearly indicates the opposite phenomenon. It is *companies* that compete and *not* business units! In fact, what will determine a business unit's ability to compete (or not compete) is determined even before that business unit is formed.

The Link between Business Unit Success and Corporate Competitiveness

Successful companies, in our view, are those that can *leverage their unique set of capabilities (driving force and areas of excellence) across the largest number of products and markets.* Companies that can spread the heartbeat of the business and their accompanying strategic capabilities across as many business units as possible are those that will assist that business unit in surviving and prospering. The opposite is also true. Business units that cannot use key corporate capabilities are often "orphaned" from the thrust of the corporation and will have difficultly making it on their own.

Examples abound. Unfortunately, most are from Japan, because business unit competition seems to be a concept that Japanese companies understand much better than their American counterparts.

For many years, Citizen has been primarily known for its watches. In the last few years, however, it has started selling floppy disk drives, laptop display screens, color TVs, and video camera viewfinders (Figure 7-1). Why would a company get involved in these seemingly unrelated businesses? The answer is simple. They all draw on Citizen's expertise, built up over the years in the watch business, around liquid crystal displays (LCDs), power-saving microcircuitry, and miniaturization. Because the watch business has gone "soft," Citizen has decided to diversify. However, it is doing so in other business arenas

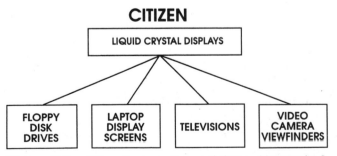

Figure 7-1. Citizen's strategic capabilities. (*Copyright © 1988 by Decision Processes International. All rights reserved.*)

where it can bring its strategic capabilities (areas of excellence) to bear.

Sharp, also of Japan, is another good example. Sharp is into LCDs for laptop computers as well as a large number of other consumer electronic devices from cordless phones, projection televisions, and fax machines to electronics diaries and calculators. It has recently introduced laser diodes for use in computers, laser printers, CD players, and videodisc players. It is working on photosensitive films that will someday function as a self-contained image-processing computer and eliminate the need for memory chips and microprocessors (Figure 7-2). Why is Sharp engaged in all these diverse product, customer, and market areas? They all draw on Sharp's knowledge of optoelectronic technology. "We've been accumulating optoelectronics know-how for 21 years" says President Haruo Tsuji in a *Business Week* article (April 29, 1991), which accounts for Sharp's success as the world's largest supplier of optoelectronic devices with sales of over $11 billion yearly.

Canon and Casio are two more Japanese examples. Canon's wide range of products—copiers, cameras, and fax machines—all draw on that company's imaging and microprocessor know-how (Figure 7-3).

The calculators, television screens, watches, and musical instruments that come from Casio all have the common trait of drawing on the company's expertise in the areas of semiconductors and digital displays (Figure 7-4).

A fifth Japanese company that clearly understands its heartbeat (driving force) is Honda. Although its most visible products

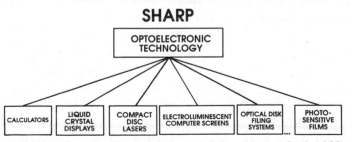

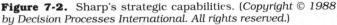

Figure 7-2. Sharp's strategic capabilities. (*Copyright © 1988 by Decision Processes International. All rights reserved.*)

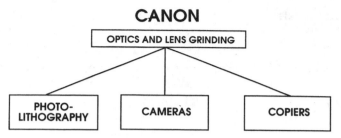

Figure 7-3. Canon's strategic capabilities. (*Copyright ©
1988 by Decision Processes International. All rights reserved.*)

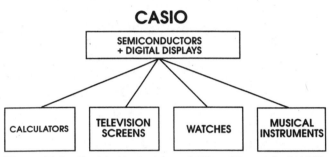

Figure 7-4. Casio's strategic capabilities. (*Copyright © 1988
by Decision Processes International. All rights reserved.*)

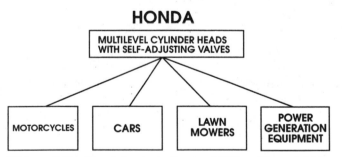

Figure 7-5. Honda's strategic capabilities. (*Copyright ©
1988 by Decision Processes International. All rights reserved.*)

are its cars, Honda also makes lawn mowers, motorcycles, and
generators (Figure 7-5). All these products revolve around
Honda's key expertise—engines—and the company is religiously
following Mr. Honda's business concept of "engines for the
world." When Honda entered Formula 1 racing, it went in with
its engines. The car bodies were by McLaren, Lotus, and others.

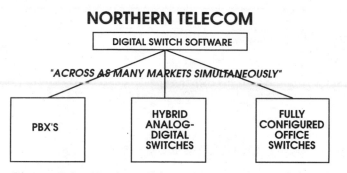

Figure 7-6. Northern Telecom's strategic capabilities. (*Copyright © 1988 by Decision Processes International. All rights reserved.*)

Canada's Northern Telecom is another company that clearly understands its strategic capability and has been exploiting it very successfully worldwide for a number of years. When Northern Telecom developed the software for its first digital switch, it did so in a manner to ensure that it would be used in a wide range of products including hybrid analog switches, configurated central office switches, and PBXs (Figure 7-6).

The news is not all bad for American companies. There are some that clearly know where their strategic advantage lies. Hewlett-Packard and 3M are two good examples. Hewlett-Packard has exploited its knowledge of instrumentation technology into everything from scientific measuring devices to oscilloscopes (Figure 7-7).

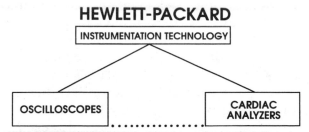

Figure 7-7. Hewlett-Packard's strategic capabilities. (*Copyright © 1988 by Decision Processes International. All rights reserved.*)

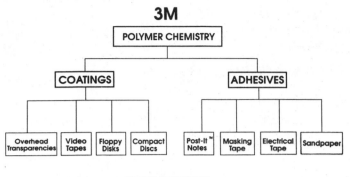

Figure 7-8. 3M's strategic capabilities. (*Copyright © 1988 by Decision Processes International. All rights reserved.*)

3M is probably the best U.S. example of a company that has built an array of some 60,000 products based on its knowledge of polymer chemistry as applied to coatings and adhesives. This strategic capability has led 3M into some 50 business arenas such as film, floppy disks, videocassettes, audiotape, sandpaper, adhesive tape, electrical tape, computer wires—to their most recent success—Post-it™ Notes (Figure 7-8).

Another CEO who clearly understands his company's strategic heartbeat and its corresponding area of excellence, and the advantage of leveraging these across all products and markets, is Percy Barnevik of ABB, the electrical equipment company based in Switzerland. Although the company sells locomotives, robotics, turbines, and power generation equipment, at the root of all these businesses is ABB's expertise in electricity and electronics—a technology-based strategy. As such, Barnevik fuels and cultivates that expertise by investing 8 percent, as compared to 5 percent by competitors, into R&D. "You have to be in command of your core technology," he says in an article appearing in *Fortune* (June 29, 1992). "For us, it's power semiconductors (electronic switching devices for high-voltage transmission), and I wouldn't dream of buying them from the Japanese." He then ensures that this capability is spread across all of ABB's businesses which is the leverage that the corporate parent brings to each of its business units.

There are also some examples of companies that do not understand what is at the root of their business. In the late 1970s and early 1980s Armco, up to that time a very successful steel company, decided to diversify. And diversify it did! Into everything from oil rigs, petroleum exploration, building products, strategic metals, and insurance. For a short time, the new strategy seemed to pay off with record profits. But in 1982 the company lost $342 million, and it is still trying to recuperate to this day. The reason: When these unrelated businesses got into trouble, Armco management, who were steel people, did not understand the unrelated businesses, and Armco itself was not bringing any strategic advantage to any of them.

Another example is United Airlines. Under its previous CEO, United negotiated cost-reduction labor contracts with its unions only to use the money to diversify into hotel and car rentals with its purchase of Hertz and Hilton—two businesses to which it brought little advantage. Even the union executive, Captain Jim Damron, understood this, when, in a *Business Week* article (May 15, 1989), he complained: "In two consecutive contracts, we gave concessions to the company, and we received nothing in exchange except seeing our company lose 25 percent of our market share. They took that economic leverage and used it to buy hotels and rental cars."

The lesson to be learned from all these examples is quite clear. The CEO and the management team must clearly understand what is the driving force of the business that constitutes its strategic weapon and competitive advantage. As one Exxon executive told this author as to why Exxon eventually retreated from its disastrous foray into office equipment: "We did not understand the `trivia' of those businesses and, therefore, could bring nothing to the table."

Understanding what component of the business is its strategic heartbeat and what are your company's strategic capabilities will greatly enhance your ability to succeed in your current markets, as well as open up other opportunities in possibly unrelated product/market areas that are strategically sound because they draw on the firm's strategic competence.

The opposite concept is also valid. Product and market opportunities that *do not* draw on the strategic capabilities of the company, as financially attractive as they may seem, will probably fail because this new business unit will not be able to draw on any key corporate skills to defend itself against competitors.

Strategic versus Operational Objectives

Another element we encountered while working with client organizations worldwide is that many people have great difficulty distinguishing between strategic and operational objectives. Most organizations, in fact, seemed to be quite competent at generating operational objectives, but few knew how to formulate strategic objectives. Understanding the difference between these is an important nuance to master if one wants a strategy to be implemented.

Let me first define *operational objectives.* In most organizations, there is an annual ritual that occurs whereby each function, or department, assembles and makes projections for the following year's revenues and costs. It then establishes for itself goals and objectives to achieve which, hopefully, are somewhat higher than the goals of the current year. The activity goes on in these and other major functions:

- Sales
- Marketing
- Manufacturing
- Accounting
- Human resources
- Research
- Customer service

Sometimes these objectives are congruent; sometimes they are not. They are all, however, extrapolations of history. People look back five years and, based on the history over that period, make adjustments for inflation and such and then extrapolate forward.

Strategic objectives are very different in nature. Strategic objectives relate to four elements of the business, each of which is a key part of the future strategic profile or vision. These elements are:

- Products
- Customer groups
- Market segments
- Geographic markets

Strategic objective is a concept that comes from the military. A strategic objective is a strategic "position" that a strategy must protect or capture. The concept is simple. In a military sense, the commander must know that of the three hills that he or she possesses on the right-hand side of the battlefield, the one on the left and the one on the right can be abandoned, but the one in the middle must be defended to the last person because from it is an unobstructed view over half the battlefield (Figure 7-9). On the other side of the battlefield, the hill on the right and in the middle are not important, but the one on the left must be captured because it will give an unobstructed view of the other half of the battlefield.

The same concept applies to business. The CEO and the management team must clearly understand which "hills" must be defended at all costs and which "hills" must be captured to win the war.

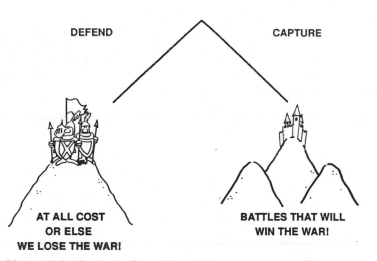

DEFEND **CAPTURE**

**AT ALL COST
OR ELSE
WE LOSE THE WAR!**

**BATTLES THAT WILL
WIN THE WAR!**

Figure 7-9. Strategic objectives are strategic positions. (*Copyright © 1987 by Decision Processes International. All rights reserved.*)

Some years ago I was a brand manager for a consumer packaged-goods firm, and I was responsible for a core product—margarine. At the time we had approximately 65 percent of the market. We, as a group, had made a conscious decision that we would never let our share drop under 60 percent. It was our view that a 60 percent share was the acceptable minimum for economies of scale on both the manufacturing and marketing sides of the business. And we had decided to defend that position against all comers. This was a strategic defensive position that was to be protected at all costs because the margarine business was considered to be the company's "crown jewels." As a result, a series of defensive tactics were automatically triggered whenever there was a one-point drop in share. Everything from additional advertising at 64 percent to special in-store merchandising programs at 63 percent to price discounts at 61 percent. These would stay in place until the competitor gave up. We defended this position for as long as it took against all comers.

On the other side, offensive strategic objectives are also formulated. They represent "new hills" that need to be captured and which will serve as signals that our strategy is working. Naturally, offensive tactics are then developed to ensure that these will materialize.

The defensive and offensive strategic objectives then become the framework for the development of operational objectives in each of the company's functions or departments. The establishment of strategic objectives is the tool required to cascade the strategy down into the ranks of the organization and to ensure congruency of goals—in other words, to ensure that everyone in the boat is rowing in the same direction.

8

Managing Your Competitor's Strategy: The General Patton Approach to Competition

There are a number of theories flourishing in the United States that revolve around competition and how one should deal with one's competitors. Here again, we have some contrary, but logical, views. Most of the theories support a perspective that one must worry about all competitors simultaneously and try to be successful against all of them. Our view is that no company has the resources or ability to compete against all competitors and should not attempt to do so. Instead, a company should target a few key competitors and ensure success against these. In fact, we are also of the opinion that, sometimes, competition is irrelevant.

To Compete or Not to Compete?

The rules of competition described in this chapter are based on the premise that a company has made the decision to grow its business at some competitor's expense. That is not always the case. Some markets may be growing at a rate sufficient to satisfy everyone's appetite. An example is the PC market during the 1980s. During that 10-year period, how much time do you think Apple spent worrying about Compaq or Compaq about Apple? Right! Probably very little, because there was plenty of growth in this market to keep both companies churning out record-breaking sales and profits year after year. However, how do you think that will change in the next 10 years? Right again. As the demand for PCs plateaus, these companies will start looking at each other for growth much more closely than before. Therefore, a major caution is that the concepts in this chapter only apply if you have made a *conscious* decision that you have to increase your business at some competitor's expense.

Once the decision to grow is made, how does one go about doing it? Once again, we find that most gurus of competitive tactics, who preach the concept of attacking a competitor's weaknesses, are wrong. We believe that a better approach is General Patton's approach:

> I have studied the enemy all my life. I have read the memoirs of his generals and his leaders. I have even read his philosophers and listened to his music. I have studied in detail the account of every damned one of his battles. I know exactly how he'll react under any given set of circumstances. And he hasn't the slightest idea what I'm going to do. So when the time comes, I'm going to whip the hell out of him.

The following are, in our view, a set of rules that will produce better results against your competition.

Rule 1: Control the "Sandbox"

The mark of a successful strategy is that it allows you to *control*, or at least *influence*, the terms of play in the "competitive sandbox." If you are not controlling or at least influencing the conditions of play in the competitive arena you have proactively chosen, your strategy is not working! Change it quickly rather than suffer a long, painful death.

For the last 30 years, IBM has controlled the terms of play in the computer area. Has Unisys? Has Honeywell? Has NEC? Has Fitjusi? Has Wang? Obviously not! Apple, Compaq, and Sun are currently trying to *influence* the terms of play. They are not yet in control, but their recent actions indicate an attempt to influence or even change the terms of play. Will they succeed? Time will tell. The remainder are not even in the sandbox.

AT&T used to control the telecommunications sandbox. Does it today? Does MCI? Probably not. Does U.S. Sprint? Definitely not. Does anybody? Probably not. Who will eventually? Time will tell. In the meantime, several players will make attempts and several will come and go before a new sandbox with clearly defined terms of play emerges.

If your strategy does not allow you to control or at least influence the terms of play in the competitive sandbox in which you have chosen to play, this is a clear signal that it's not working! Change it because it's a reactive strategy. Otherwise you will always be reacting to events created by other companies.

Rule 2: Identify Which Competitors Your Strategy Will Attract

Once your strategy has been developed, look around to see which organizations will be attracted to it. If your strategy represents a change from the one you pursued in the past, the competitors it will attract will *not* be the same as the previous ones. Once you understand your strategy, and the sandbox you will be in, new potential competitors can easily be identified.

Rule 3: Anticipate Each Potential Competitor's Future Strategy

The next step is to anticipate each competitor's driving force and business concept. At this point, some might say that this cannot be done because we do not sit in on our competitor's strategy sessions. However, the strategy of any company ends up translating itself into physical evidence such as products, geographic markets, customers, buildings, technologies, facilities, people, skills, and so forth. By looking at the actions of a competitor in these areas, one can identify what has *driven* the competitor to do what it has done—in other words, identify what was the driving force behind that competitor's strategy. In the same manner, by looking at a competitor's current actions, announced actions, or anticipated actions, one can identify the strategic heartbeat of that competitor's business. This can be done for each competitor that you think your strategy will attract.

Rule 4: Draw Competitive Profiles

You can now anticipate where each competitor will put its emphasis and de-emphasis in terms of products, users, and geographic markets; therefore, you can now draw "pictures" of what each competitor will look like from the pursuit of such a strategy. One misconception exists, however, about competitive behavior. Many people assume that all the competitors in one industry behave the same way. Not necessarily so. Usually, each competitor's strategic heartbeat is different, so each competitor will act differently under a similar set of circumstances. However, if you detect what is at the root of a competitor's strategy, you can anticipate the various behaviors and put into place a different set of actions to deal with each competitor. For example, although Toyota and Honda are both in the car industry, each will react very differently under a similar set of circumstances because each is pursuing a strategy that has a different driving force at its root. Toyota wants to become "the world's largest car company," whereas Honda's driving force is its engine technology; it is in the car business only because of Mr. Honda's concept of producing "engines for the world."

Other examples are Kimberly-Clark and Procter & Gamble. Both companies are slugging it out in the diaper business with their Huggies and Pampers brands (Figure 8-1). Although they find themselves fierce competitors in this arena, each is there for a radically different reason. Kimberly-Clark is there because the driving force of its strategy is to optimize the *capacity* of its paper mills. And one arena where this can be done is in the baby diaper market. Procter & Gamble, on the other hand, has a strategy with

COMPETITIVE BEHAVIOR IS PREDICTABLE

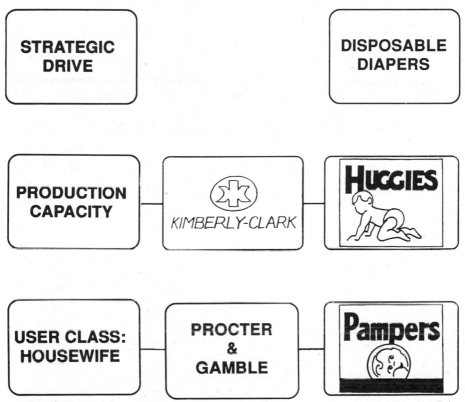

STRATEGIC DRIVE

DISPOSABLE DIAPERS

PRODUCTION CAPACITY — KIMBERLY-CLARK — HUGGIES

USER CLASS: HOUSEWIFE — PROCTER & GAMBLE — Pampers

Figure 8-1. *(Copyright © 1982 by Decision Processes International. All rights reserved. Revised 1990.)*

a very different driving force at its root: "Meeting the household needs of *housewives*" (a user class–driven strategy), has been at the root of the company since its conception. It is in the diaper market because diapers represent one such need.

Under a similar set of circumstances, each of these companies will behave very differently. Let us suppose that a third company, such as Du Pont, were to invent a synthetic fiber ten times as absorbent as cellulose. How would Kimberly-Clark and Procter & Gamble behave?

Procter & Gamble would sell off its paper mills and buy the new fiber because it would not let go of its consumer and strategic heartbeat—the homemaker/mother. On the other hand, Kimberly-Clark would probably ease out of the business and seek other opportunities that might employ cellulose and the capacity of its mills. It would give up the homemaker rather than its paper mills.

Understanding what is at the root of a company's strategy can help you predict that company's behavior under a given set of variables. Honda, again, is another example. When faced with emission control standards imposed on the industry by the EPA in the 1970s, all other car companies responded with catalytic converters. Not Honda! Honda went back to work on what drives its business and what it knows best—engine technology—and it redesigned its engine to meet the EPA's standards without the need for a catalytic converter.

Rule 5: Manage the Competitor's Strategy

Not so long ago, we had the opportunity to work with one of the best known manufacturers of buses. When we arrived, one competitor was identified as pursuing a "copycat" strategy. In other words, whatever bus contract our client bid on, a few weeks later its competitor would enter a similar but lower-price bid. If our client chose not to bid, neither would the competitor. The pattern repeated itself all over the world. Once the competitor's strategy was recognized, a plan was developed to "manage" that strategy. A very large project emerged in Asia involving some 4000 buses. Because of a previous bad experience in that part of the world, our client did not want the project. However, to lure the competitor, the company put in a bid that included more services than required and at a price well below cost. Sure enough, the competitor submitted a bid and was awarded the contract. Two-thirds of the way into the project, the competitor ran into major cost overruns to the extent that the company announced it was looking for a merger partner to help it out of financial difficulties. A little later, our client bought out its competitor for a song, took over its market, and eliminated it from others. All actions were put into place *two years before!*

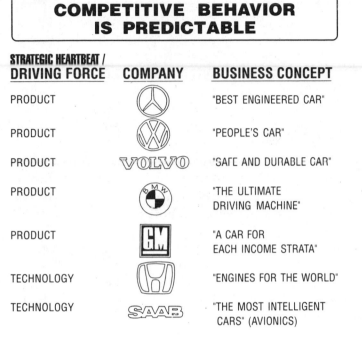

COMPETITIVE BEHAVIOR IS PREDICTABLE

STRATEGIC HEARTBEAT / DRIVING FORCE	COMPANY	BUSINESS CONCEPT
PRODUCT	Mercedes-Benz	"BEST ENGINEERED CAR"
PRODUCT	Volkswagen	"PEOPLE'S CAR"
PRODUCT	VOLVO	"SAFE AND DURABLE CAR"
PRODUCT	BMW	"THE ULTIMATE DRIVING MACHINE"
PRODUCT	GM	"A CAR FOR EACH INCOME STRATA"
TECHNOLOGY	Honda	"ENGINES FOR THE WORLD"
TECHNOLOGY	SAAB	"THE MOST INTELLIGENT CARS" (AVIONICS)

Figure 8-2. *(Copyright © 1988 by Decision Processes International. All rights reserved. Revised 1990.)*

If one wants to identify a competitor's strategy, one needs to understand two elements about that competitor. These two elements are the competitor's driving force (strategic heartbeat) and the business concept that the competitor is practicing in that mode. Again, let us look at the car industry for examples (Figure 8-2).

In the car industry, as noted before, several companies are pursuing a product concept–driven strategy. For example, Mercedes-Benz's concept of its product is the "best engineered car." It's a concept articulated by Karl Benz some 110 years ago and has propelled this company ever since, resulting in uninterrupted profits year after year, in spite of what is happening in the automobile wars. This concept, therefore, determines how the car looks, whom it is sold to, how it is merchandised, how it is priced, and so on.

Then along comes Volkswagen, also a product concept–driven company—cars and more cars and more cars. However,

Volkswagen's concept, as we all know, is slightly different from Mercedes'. As first articulated by Dr. Porsche, VWs are a "people's car." As such, Volkswagen goes down a slightly different road than Mercedes, starting with how the car looks, whom it is sold to, how it is priced, how it is merchandised, and so on.

Then along comes Volvo, again, a product concept–driven company. Its concept—"safe and durable" cars—is different still and is the concept articulated by the founders of the company, Gustaf Larson and Assar Gabrielsson, back in 1927. They believed that the most important thing a carmaker could offer its customers was a safe trip. As a result, Volvo's product has a slightly different look, is sold to a slightly different customer, at slightly different prices, and so on. In other words, Volvo goes down yet a slightly different road.

Then along comes BMW, another product concept–driven company. Because of its slightly different business concept—the "ultimate driving machine"—BMW's cars are sold on their performance capabilities.

Then comes General Motors. What is GM's business concept? In order to identify the business concept, it is sometimes necessary to go back into the company's history. In this instance, one has to start with Alfred Sloan, who articulated GM's concept in the 1920s as "a car for each income strata." The concept then stated: "As such, GM cars must look distinguishable one from the other" to justify a higher price as Americans migrated up the income scale and bought a higher-priced GM car.

Here is a good example of why it is important to understand the business concept of an enterprise. During the 1970s GM was attacked by the Japanese. In response, GM management, faced with mounting losses of market share, took a quick look at Japanese carmakers to determine what advantage they had and concluded that it was cheap labor—which resulted in a $1500 per car price advantage. Therefore, GM said, we must reduce our costs. Therefore, we must have all our cars go through the same manufacturing system. Therefore, what do we do with the design? Right! We must make all of our cars' designs similar.

When GM went down the "look-alike" road in the mid-1970s, its management lost sight of GM's original business concept, which had contributed to its success through the years. Ford, on the other hand, used to have a "copycat GM" strategy from 1940 to 1975. Whatever models GM brought out, Ford would copy within a year or so. In the mid-1970s, however, when Ford executives saw GM go down the "look-alike" road, Ford finally said "not this time." Then Ford—not GM—started making "distinguishable looking cars." In fact Ford today is practicing GM's strategy; Ford has inherited GM's strategy by default because GM management abandoned it by accident! And who has had more success against those same Japanese competitors in the 1980s? You're right! Ford...by billions of dollars. Which leads us to another conclusion about strategy: *The strategy of a business can change by accident when management loses sight of the underlying business concept of the enterprise.*

So far, the preceding examples are all related to companies that are pursuing a product concept–driven strategy. But as you will have noted, each has a slightly different concept of its product that will lead the company to behave differently given the same circumstance.

Another error of the competitive gurus is preaching that all the competitors in a given industry behave in the same manner, and, therefore, that the factors of success are the same for everybody. We have never found that to be true. Instead, our work indicates that although several competitors may share the same driving force, business concepts will be different enough for each company to behave in a slightly different manner given the same circumstance. *And that behavior can be anticipated* if one understands each competitor's driving force and business concept and if one can manage that competitor's strategy to one's advantage.

To avoid another flaw in the competitor gurus' thinking, never accept that all competitors in a given industry have the same driving force. Here are two more examples.

Honda is in the car business. But what is Honda's driving force? As shown in the General Motors example offered earlier, identifying a competitor's business concept sometimes calls for one to look back into that company's history. On other occasions, however, one needs to look at what other product categories the competitor is into beyond those with which your division or company is meeting in the marketplace. Honda makes cars, but it also makes motorcycles, lawn mowers, and generators. What is common to all these products? *Engines.* And if one were to read *Memoirs,* written by the now-deceased Mr. Honda, one would find his business concept: "Engines for the world." Honda is only in the car business because cars require engines. If someone ever invented a car that did not require an engine, Honda would soon exit that business. This concept also explains Mr. Honda's refusal to follow MITI's (Japan's Ministry of International Trade and Industry) suggestion in the 1960s not to enter the car business because Japan already had too many car manufacturers. Understanding the concept, however, helps one to understand Honda's behavior in the marketplace. It explains, for example, Honda's desire to enter Formula 1 racing—only the engine portion, mind you, not the body. One can also explain Honda's behavior when faced with competitive threats.

In the 1970s, the EPA announced strict emission control standards for cars. What did all the product concept–driven companies do? Add a catalytic converter to the engine. Not Honda. Honda went back to its driving force—engine technology—and changed its engine to meet the new standards without the need for a catalytic convertor. In 1991, Honda did it again. Threatened with a new set of standards in California in 1995, Honda has developed an engine that already meets those standards without the need for additional components. Rest assured that Honda will spread that technology across all of its other products quickly, thus leveraging its driving force and strategic heartbeat. To prove our point that competitive behavior is predictable, one might wonder where else Honda might apply its engine technology know-how. This author is prepared to predict Honda's eventual entry into aircraft engines. Watch out Rolls Royce and Pratt & Whitney!

A last example is Saab. Saab is also in the car business. But what is Saab's driving force and business concept? Again, in what other business is Saab? The answer—military aircraft. Saab's roots are based in this area and Saab's business concept, as articulated by its founder, wants to prove "what allied aircraft philosophy can do for your car driving." As a result, if a competitor attacks Saab, Saab would respond by putting a turbo engine in the back of the car, fins on the side of the car, and a cockpit in the driver's seat!

The thrust of all the preceding examples is simple:

- Each competitor within a given industry is there for a slightly different reason.

- To understand the competitor's strategy for being there, one needs to identify each competitor's driving force and business concept.
- Once that is understood, one can do things to manage the competitor's strategy to one's advantage.

Rule 6: Neutralize the Competitor's Areas of Excellence

A *proactive* strategy is one that allows you to control or influence the rules of play in the competitive sandbox. Some experts will tell you that the way to do this is to analyze each competitor's strengths and weaknesses and then to exploit those weaknesses. Time and again, while working in strategy sessions with successful CEOs, this did not usually hold much appeal. When asked "Why not?" one CEO replied, "I'm not interested in spending *my* money to make any competitor stronger." When asked to clarify this statement, he went on to explain that attacking a competitor's weakness makes the competitor recognize this weakness and then do things to correct or eliminate it. You have awakened the competitor to that weakness, gained a competitive edge temporarily, but then given the competitor a long-term advantage. You now need to attack another weakness and the whole cycle starts over. If you carry this scenario to its logical but somewhat absurd end, eventually you will have strengthened your competitor so much that it might put you out of business.

A better way, in our opinion, to deal with competitors is to anticipate each competitor's strategy and then manage that strategy, which will put you in a stronger competitive position. This, as mentioned earlier, is not achieved by attacking a competitor's weakness or by attacking a competitor's many strengths. Managing a competitor's strategy and controlling the sandbox can only be achieved by attacking the driving force of the competitor's strategy and accompanying areas of excellence.

Remember that an area of excellence is a describable skill or capability that a company deliberately cultivates over time, to a degree of proficiency higher than anything else it does but, more important, better than any competitor does. It is this higher degree of competence in a couple of key strategic skills that keeps the company's strategic heartbeat strong and healthy and gives it an edge against its competitors. Areas of excellence are to the strategy of a business what clean arteries are to the human heart. When the arteries get plugged up, the heart stops beating. When one's strategic skills diminish, then the strategy loses its strength and, thus, its edge against its competitors. Here are three examples. One trait that most customers recognize in IBM is the company's superior customer service. In fact, it is during times when IBM does not have the best computers that this key strategic skill keeps its customers loyal. IBM knows this and invests in deliberately developing this skill. Fred Smith at Federal Express says that his company's area of excellence is its ability to "track, trace, and control" packages in its distribution system better than any competitor. Shell Oil claims that its ability to find oil at depths of "1200 feet or below" is its competitive advantage.

The strategy of any company is supported by the development of expertise or skills in a couple of strategic areas, and it is these areas of excellence that make that company's strategy work. Therefore, the same concept applies in reverse. If you want to weaken a competitor's strategy, attack that competitor's areas of excellence. Diluting, diminishing, or neutralizing those areas of excellence is the best way in which you can obtain a significant advantage and control or influence the sandbox. You attack the heart and guts of the business. You attack the strategic heartbeat and key strategic skills of that competitor. You go for the throat. There is no such thing as genteel competition. The Japanese, for example, attacked at the heart of American automobile companies' businesses—they made better cars!

When MCI decided that it needed to be more aggressive at AT&T's expense, it chose not to exploit AT&T's weaknesses, but to attack AT&T's heartbeat. "MCI is starting to hurt AT&T where it hurts the most: the Big Business customer" reported in the September 18, 1989, issue of *Time* magazine. "MCI is determined to steal the giant's bread and butter accounts." MCI went after AT&T's largest account—Merrill Lynch—and won. Next on MCI's hit list: Chrysler, United Airlines, Westinghouse, and Procter & Gamble.

Another example is U.S. Surgical. Its CEO, Leon Hirsh, who

masterminded the revolution to surgical staples from the traditional needles and thread, has now decided to enter a new arena, that of medical sutures—Johnson & Johnson territory. As the August 7, 1989, issue of *Business Week* reported: "He's going after their lifeblood" because sutures contribute 10 percent of Johnson & Johnson's total earnings.

A third example comes from the computer industry. After years of making cheaper IBM mainframe clones and being relatively successful, a May 1991 article in *Business* reports that Fujitsu has decided to go "right to the heart of Big Blue's territory: mainframe computers." But instead of clones, this time Fujitsu will manufacture the "advanced microchips vital for future generations of machines, something no other American computer maker, except IBM, can do." This strategy will result, not in cheaper clones, but in better machines that will be designed to outperform IBM's.

These three examples illustrate what I call the Vince Lombardi school of management. When Lombardi's football teams took to the field, the first six plays were directed, not at the opponent's weaknesses, but at its strengths. Prior to each game, Lombardi analyzed his opponent and identified the best four players on its defense. His offensive plan was then directed at these four players—the heartbeat of the opponent's defense. The rationale was simple. If his team broke through in those first few plays, the game was over! By attacking a competitor's weaknesses, the game gets played between the 40-yard lines. Up 10 yards, back 10 yards. If one wants to get to the end zone to score, one needs to attack at the heart of the opponent's defense. The same is true in business. Attacking a competitor's weaknesses only leads to marginal changes in market position. Significant gains can only be made by attacking the heartbeat of that competitor's strategy.

Once you have identified your competitor's future driving force and translated it into a profile of products, markets, and customers resulting from that strategy, you need to identify the areas of excellence that each competitor is cultivating to support that strategy. These will be different from one competitor to another because each company is probably pursing a different strategy. Once this has been done, you are ready to proceed to determining which sandbox you want to play in.

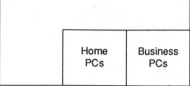

The IBM Sandbox

Mainframes	Micros	Minis
Laptops	PCs	Software

Figure 8-3.

The Compaq Sandbox

	Home PCs	Business PCs

Figure 8-4.

Rule 7: Choose Your Competitors; Do Not Let Your Competitors Choose You

To be proactive, each company must consciously choose in which competitive arena, or "sandbox," it wants to be. The first step is to delimit the sandbox. You can make the sandbox as large or as small as you want. It's your choice. IBM has chosen to compete in all corners of the computer sandbox, from laptops to mainframes (Figure 8-3). Compaq, on the other hand, has decided to limit the size of its sandbox to PCs. In fact, it has even decided to divide this sandbox even further into home PCs and business PCs (Figure 8-4). Compaq's strategy is to deliberately avoid the home PC market because of its volatility.

Once you have delimited the sandbox you wish to play in, you need to ask: Who do we invite into the sandbox to have a good time with?

All successful CEOs we have worked with were always careful not to be drawn into competitive arenas by mistake. In order to "control" the sandbox and the terms of play, two decisions must be made. The first is to choose which competitor to invite into the sandbox because you are confident that you can attack that competitor's strategic heartbeat and areas of excellence. Against this competitor, you now want to devise "offensive" tactics to accomplish this objective. We will discuss how to do this in the next chapter. The second class of competitors to include in your sandbox are those that are in a position of attacking your areas of excellence. You'll want to monitor these competitors very carefully because they could give your strategy difficulty. The rest of the competitors are probably not in a position to do much damage. If you don't disturb them, they probably will not disturb you. If any attack you, they will probably attack your weaknesses and only make you better.

In our view, one should practice the concept we call *single target* competition. In other words, go after *one* competitor at a time. We all know what happens to someone who starts a war on two fronts! Again, the Japanese are masters of this concept.

Toyota, since its inception, has had only one competitor in its sight—General Motors. Toyota's stated strategy is to outsell GM worldwide and, eventually, in the United States. Komatsu has had only one competitor in its sight for over 30 years. Not Deere, not Fiat, not Volvo—but Caterpillar. Komatsu's strategic war cry is "Eat the Cat." At Honda, the war cry is "Beat Benz," not in terms of the number of cars sold, but in terms of the quality of cars built. And for the last three years, Honda has achieved its goal.

Subaru has recently targeted Volvo. For many years, Volvo's strategy has been to build "safe and durable" cars, and for the last 20 years Volvo has been showing us pictures of its cars crashing into walls and the passengers walking away uninjured. Subaru has recently started an advertising campaign that, at the top of the page, shows the Volvo car crashed into the wall and, at the bottom of the page, a Subaru car stopped one yard from the wall. The caption: "If you want to be in an accident, buy a Volvo. If you want to prevent an accident, buy a Subaru." Subaru has targeted Volvo and has decided not to attack Volvo's weaknesses, but rather the very heartbeat of its strategy. And Subaru has come up with a very ingenious way to do this. In just six months, Subaru started to make significant gains at Volvo's expense.

In the Gulf War of 1991, General Schwarzkopf's quick victory can be attributed to his study of General Patton's concepts. Even before the war began, Brigadier General Richard Neal noted during one of his briefings, as reported in the December 9, 1991, issue of *Forbes*: "We are inside his (Saddam Hussein) decision-making cycle. We can see what he's been doing, we can anticipate what his next move is going to [be], and we can adapt our tactics accordingly." As a result of having anticipated Hussein's strategy, Schwarzkopf refused to oblige him by engaging in a war on Hussein's terms; instead, Schwarzkopf did everything to confuse Hussein and encountered almost no resistance when his own plan went into effect.

Changing the Rules of Play

Our experience with corporations has made us firm believers in General Patton's approach to competition. In fact, the concept is even older than General Patton. A Chinese General, Sun Tzu, wrote in the fourth century that "what is of supreme importance in war is to attack the enemy's strategy." And the best way to neutralize a competitor's strategic heartbeat, in our view, is to *change the rules of play*.

9

Changing the Rules of Play

Many theories have emerged over the years about how to grow one's business at a competitor's expense. Once you have identified your competitor's areas of excellence—because it is not wise to attack weaknesses—you might conclude that the best way to grow is to "out excel" the competitor. In other words, attempt to be better than the competition in the capabilities that the competitor does best. However, all one is doing in this approach is entering a race with no finish line. One competitor surges ahead of the other for a short period of time only to be overtaken by another competitor for another period of time, to then regain the lead for another period of time, to...I think you see what I mean. A race with no end—and no *winner!*

In fact, if there is to be a winner, it probably will be the competitor with the largest market share. In other words, the competitor that started the race in the first place is more than likely to have greater lasting power than the rest of the field in this type of game. It's somewhat akin to playing poker with someone that has 10 times the bankroll you have. He or she will eventually wear you out. We have come to discourage this concept of competition, especially if you are number 2, 3, or 4 in the market.

Our experience has shown that if you are not the leader, *never play the game according to the rules the leader has set*. Otherwise, you are certain to lose! In other words, do not try to "out excel" the competitor in its areas of excellence or strategic capabilities. Playing by the rules set by the leader in an industry is certain death over time. The leader understands the rules better—it designed them. The leader can enforce them more effectively; it has more resources to do so. And the leader will crush you!

A better approach, in our view, is to *change the rules of play*. By changing the rules of play, you *neutralize* and *paralyze* the leader. While the leader is temporarily immobilized and on the sidelines, you can make significant gains against that competitor.

Examples of Companies That Have Changed the Rules

One of the first companies to introduce a paper copier was 3M. But within a few years, 3M was out of the copier business. During our consulting work with 3M, we asked some of their executives to explain what had happened. 3M, they said, sold their machines to their customers. Xerox introduced its copiers and started *leasing* them to its customers. The 3M executives could not figure out how Xerox could make money leasing machines. All the equations they used on leasing as an option turned out red ink. Model after model, time after time. 3M could not bring itself to understand the leasing business. As a result they were paralyzed, sat on the sidelines, and watched as Xerox took the market away. Xerox had changed the rules of play!

A few years later, Canon came into the market with its copiers and changed the rules of play again. Xerox sold its machines through a direct sales force. Canon started selling through distributors. While Xerox sat on the sidelines paralyzed, Canon gained a significant share of Xerox's market.

A company that has had considerable success in a very mundane business over the last 20 years is Domino's Pizza. And most of that success was achieved by changing the rules of play. Thomas Monaghan, founder of Domino's, invented the concept of "guaranteed home delivery within 30 minutes." This guarantee was possible because of the development of a special envelope around the pizza to keep it warm during the delivery. As a result, Domino's has grown to several thousand outlets with almost no reply from its competitors.

In the stock brokerage business, Charles Schwab has grown a very successful business from scratch by also changing the rules to his advantage. The firm's net revenues have risen to over $500 million, and its stock price has gone from $7 to $33—by not doing what other brokers do. Schwab's personnel are on salary versus commission, they take calls 24 hours per day on three shifts versus a one-shift day for its competitors, and 20 percent of its business comes from an automated system rather than through direct phone contact with a broker. As a result, Schwab has challenged and changed the most important rule of the industry: Schwab's commission rates are less than half of the traditional houses!

In Europe, another upstart is making substantial gains at its competitor's expenses by changing the rules of play. Martin Carver, CEO of Bandag, Inc.—a tire retreading company—decided that his business could not grow by emulating his competitors. Instead of working through its own distribution system, as it had done for decades, Carver dismantled the company in favor of a franchise system that costs each franchisee $150,000. Unlike its competitors, which insist that customers come to the retreader's shop, Bandag franchisees come to the customer's premises in specially designed $60,000 trucks filled with tires and equipment. Furthermore, the trucks are sent out after hours so that the customer's business is not interrupted. The result? Bandag's share has grown from 5 to 20 percent in Europe and now accounts for 18 percent of the company's total business, as compared to 5 percent in the 1980s.

In the health-care business, another company is succeeding by changing the rules of play to its favor. Employee Benefit Plans (EBP) has grown at a rate of over 30 percent per year for the last eight years by not playing the game the same way the other players do. Instead of having its customer's companies manage their health-care programs through the purchase of insurance from insurance companies, EBP shows its customers how to manage their health-care programs themselves, without the need of the insurance company and at a lower cost. As a result, EBP is now a $250 million company and soon to be much larger.

JCB, a U.K. manufacturer of backhoe loaders, has seen its business grow from $200 million to over $1 billion also by changing the rules of play on its bigger heavy machinery competitors. It has achieved this by giving its potential customer a trial run with its machines. Not a small marketing risk considering that each machine is worth around $80,000. But this practice, unique to JCB, has increased its share of market from approximately 180 units a year to over 2500 units in 10 years.

In the cosmetic industry, Anita Roddick has seen her company—Body Shop International—grow from nothing to over $200 million of business annually by breaking all the rules that the larger companies play by. Instead of using expensive packaging, as its chief competitors do, Body Shop utilizes plain, nondescript material. In an industry that spends millions on advertising, Body Shop spends nothing. In an industry that sells primarily through drug and department stores, Body Shop sells through exclusive franchisees. Its growth is consistently in the double digits, and its net profit is over 30 percent of sales!

Other examples abound. In the media world, Ted Turner has built CNN into a major player by not playing according to the rules set by the three big networks—ABC, CBS, and NBC. Instead of scheduling a wide variety of different types of programs, he chose to concentrate on television news, 24 hours a day. Instead of using the standard broadcast system, he chose to go with cable. Instead of playing entirely to the American domestic market, he went global. In other words, he set new rules. In an interview with *Success* magazine appearing in the Jan./Feb. 1991, issue, Turner reinforced this notion. "Have I confounded expectations?" he asked testily. "Founding TBS Superstation, CNN, TNT, Headline News. Buying the Atlanta Braves, MGM, holding the Goodwill Games. Yes. I've gone against expectations. I'm not a renegade—I'm a revolutionary."

In yet another industry, steel, a group of upstarts are in the process of changing the rules of play and creating major headaches for the traditional giants such as U.S. Steel, Inland, and Armco. New entrants such as Nucor and Chaparral are using "minimills," which represents a complete rethink of the steel fabricating process. Instead of making steel from ore that requires expensive coke ovens and blast furnaces, the minimill employs less costly electric furnaces that melt down scrap metal. As one executive of Chaparral Steel said to *Fortune* magazine in a July 1991 article: "We're Big Steel's worst nightmare, and we're not going away."

In the trucking industry, Don Schneider, CEO of Schneider National, has equipped each truck with a computer and a rotating antenna. This allows him to keep track of each truck's precise location at any point in time, as well as be able to redirect the trucks to respond to clients' requests more rapidly than any competitor. Confronted with some dramatic changes facing the trucking industry—mainly deregulation—most other companies lowered rates in an attempt to keep customers. Schneider opted to find a unique way to respond more quickly to customer needs and to maintain price and margins by providing more value.

Another revolutionary is CEO Marty Wygod of Medco Containment Services. Wygod is changing the rules of the retail drugstore business by providing companies with prescription drugs through the mail instead of through retail drugstores. The effect is a substantially lower per unit cost for the customer. The result? Medco is a $1.3 billion company and expects to double its revenues in the next five years.

Still another company that is attempting to change the rules of play is NCR. After years of playing in the computer sandbox the way IBM and the others have played, NCR has finally decided to try to change the rules. In its latest strategy, NCR has decided to give up playing the game with "boxes" and has decided to attach its future to microprocessors instead of mainframes. The strategy is based on the concept of neutralizing mainframes by linking together hundreds of microchips, thus making the mainframe almost impotent. NCR has a better chance with this strategy than with trying to take on IBM in the mainframe business. Moreover, it will be difficult for IBM to counteract because IBM has a significantly larger installed base of mainframes than NCR and is heavily dependent on that revenue base. In other words, IBM is tied to the "old" rules and may be paralyzed for a period of time while it tries to decide what to do. NCR's approach has so much appeal that even AT&T became interested, as evidenced by its takeover. No wonder AT&T fought so hard to acquire NCR. AT&T may finally have found a way to make significant inroads into IBM's turf.

Even Gillette, the inventor of the razor blade, has decided that the only way to grow its business again is to "change the playing field," as Colman Mockler stated to *Forbes* in an interview appearing in the February 4, 1991, issue. After having followed the crowd during most of the 1980s by trying to sell disposable razors and not doing very well at it because of the commodity, low price, low margin, low profit attributes of this approach, Gillette decided it "had to change the playing field. Gillette had to convince consumers to pay more for systems instead of buying cheap disposables." And thus, its introduction of the Sensor razor and blade system, which has been a phenomenal success even at $3.30 each versus a $.40 disposable, not to mention the endless need for replacement blades at $.70 apiece. In one swoop, Gillette went from a low margin business to a high margin business with an automatic multiplier to boot!

Dell Computer is still another example. Instead of marketing computers through stores, as the rules of the industry would dictate, a brash 19-year-old Texan, Michael Dell, decided to market computers using direct marketing techniques. The result: an $800 million company after only five years, one that is still going strong even during the recession of the early 1990s.

Dell has succeeded not only in the United States by changing the marketing rules there, but it is in the process of doing the same in Europe. After having been told by all the so-called marketing experts in Europe that Europeans would never buy computers through the mail, Dell decided to go ahead anyway. Guess what? Dell's business in Europe is fast approaching the $200 million mark. In fact, Dell's success is causing all the existing makers of PCs to rethink their approach to the marketing of their own products. The company that changed the rules may soon see its new rules become the industry standard, which shows that sometimes one can be so successful by changing the rules that an entire industry might feel threatened enough to convert to the new way of playing the game. Digital Equipment Corporation has already announced that it is making the plunge into direct marketing of its new line of PCs.

In the airline industry, the fastest growing and consistently most profitable company over the last 10 years is not one of the big three—American, United, or Delta—but Southwest. From nothing 10 years ago to $1.2 billion in 1991, it did this by not play-ing by the market leaders' rules. Unlike the big three, Southwest does not use a hub-and-spoke system, it flies point to point. Furthermore, it does not issue advance boarding cards, it does not serve meals, it does not take other carriers' tickets, and it does not transfer luggage to other carriers. It plays by its own rules, and it has the big three worried. As Robert Crandall, CEO of American, recently stated in a *Business Week* interview (July 6, 1992): "Southwest will be as big as we are." Why? Because by changing the rules, Southwest has the big three paralyzed. With the massive computer infrastructure the big three have built to gain an edge in their reservation systems, eliminating boarding passes to match Southwest doesn't remove any costs from the system. In other words, the big three are paralyzed and "on the sideline." During this paralysis, Southwest is making significant gains at their expense.

In the United Kingdom, an entrepreneur is in the midst of changing the rules about how books are marketed. Tim Waterstone, the founder of Waterstone Booksellers, has intro-duced the concept of bookstores with over 100,000 titles—com-pared to the W. H. Smith stores, which carry less than half that number. Furthermore, Waterstone's stores are open until 9 p.m. every night including Saturdays and Sundays, a practice unheard of in the United Kingdom. Since 1983, Waterstone Booksellers has grown to 85 stores and has opened the first of several U.S. stores in 1991.

Eyelab is a good example of a company that has changed the rules of play in order to make significant gains at its competitors expense. In order to reduce the waiting time for new eyeglasses, it transferred the manufacturing process from a single, centrally located laboratory to minilabs at each of its stores. Every Eyelab store has its own lenses, frames, grinding equipment, and techni-cians who can provide customers with eyeglasses within one hour instead of two weeks.

Sam Walton, the founder of Wal-Mart (but now deceased), was an entrepreneur who succeeded in dethroning Sears as the largest retailer in the United States. In just 30 years, his company went from nothing to $44 billion in sales to displace Sears, which had been around much longer and enjoyed sales in the billions before

Wal-Mart was even conceived. How did Walton do it? Simply by breaking all the rules that Sears had invented. For example, instead of periodic sales, Walton introduced the concept of everyday discount prices; instead of concentrating in large metropolitan areas, he built his stores in small towns that others scorned. By the time Sears woke up to the threat, Wal-Mart's momentum was unstoppable.

Sometimes, changing the rules of play puts an entire industry in jeopardy. Such is the case currently in the pharmaceutical industry. The giants—Merck, Hoffmann LaRoche, Squibb, Bristol-Myers, Sandoz, Ciba-Geigy, and others—are being challenged by a number of upstarts such as Genentech, Genzyme, Immunex, and Amgen. What do these upstarts have in common? They have changed the rules of play in regard to the process of drug development. Whereas the traditional companies have their roots in chemistry, the challengers have their roots in biology. As *Fortune* reported in the August 12, 1991, issue:

> The conventional chemical approach which still dominates drug development at the big houses, relies on hit-or-miss screenings of thousands of compounds in hopes of finding one that has medicinal properties. Only one out of 10,000 winds up on the market.
>
> By contrast, the biotech approach starts with substances the body already manufactures, either to heal directly or to act as signals that mobilize the response to an intruder. Biotech companies analyze the structure of these compounds, which are large protein molecules. Then they use genetic engineering to copy them. With the biotech approach a remarkable one of every ten possibilities has proved out.

Other advantages in the areas of costs, speed of development, and effectiveness have industry experts worried that the traditional approach will not match these new rules. Thus, they question the ability of the conventional, chemically based companies to survive in the mid-to-long term.

In Japan, a market that many companies claim is closed to foreign firms, one company is doing spectacularly well by changing the rules of play. That company, Amway, has been growing at a rate of 30 percent per year since 1979 for a total of $1 billion, one-third of the company's total revenues. How has Amway done this? By bypassing Japan's vaunted, closed, and entrenched multitiered distribution system and going direct through a sales force of one million Japanese—one-tenth of that country's population—who sell product door-to-door. So much for those who claim the market is impenetrable.

ReMax is the last corporate example we will describe, although many more exist. In the real estate business, most sales are transacted by salespeople affiliated with large retail chains such as Coldwell Banker, Merrill Lynch, Prudential, and Century 21. Most small, independent brokers are being gobbled up by these giants of the industry—except for ReMax. ReMax is a chain of independent real estate salespeople who are in the top 10 percentile of the industry in terms of productivity, who pay their own rent, who do their own advertising, and who keep a larger share of their fees. ReMax is growing at twice the rate of the larger chains.

What Happens When You Play by Another's Rules

To illustrate how dangerous it can be to play by rules set by a larger competitor, let me use the example of a French television network called La Cinq. La Cinq came into being after the French government loosened control of the media in 1986. It blossomed initially by providing a large dose of American soap operas, something unheard of in France until them.

Unfortunately, the French government regulated the number of advertising minutes the network could sell, seven per hour, which did not generate enough revenue for the network to break even. It needed to attract more viewers in an attempt to increase its rates to advertisers. In a desperate attempt to draw viewers from its larger competitor TF1, La Cinq's management decided to adopt TF1's formula of expensive, live variety shows. Unfortunately, viewers did not switch and La Cinq stopped broadcasting on April 12, 1992.

Another similar example also comes from Europe, this time England. The victim is *Punch* magazine. From 1841 to 1988 *Punch* carved out a very profitable niche for itself by playing to its own rules. It built a strong following among mid-40, university-educated, upper-middle-class readers. Its winning formula was an editorial mixture of highly literate but outrageous humor.

In 1988, a new editor decided to change that strategy and start playing the game according to other competitors' rules. Noting that a number of new magazines had sprung up catering to a younger reader, the editorial was changed to appeal to this group. Unfortunately, the other competitors knew the rules better. Not only did *Punch* not attract the younger reader, it soon saw its traditional readers abandon it in droves. In 1992, *Punch* closed its doors for good.

Playing the game according to the leader's rules can also be deadly. In an article about CEOs who are revolutionizing their industries by radically changing the rules of play to their advantage appearing in the July 15, 1991, issue, *Fortune* concluded that the CEOs succeeded by using some of the following strategies.

- Revolutionary companies have extremely sensitive antennae for the technological or market forces that create change. They look beyond what their customers say they want today to what they will need tomorrow—and what technology will permit them to have.

- These companies have a clearly defined mission—frequently and unambiguously voiced by the top brass. Knowing exactly what they are trying to do, the companies have no trouble judging which activities fit with their strategic focus and which don't.

- They use computer technology extensively, but in a highly disciplined way that demonstrably advances their strategic goals. They don't go on technology binges—for instance, as GM did when it profligately invested in robotics, in EDS, and in Hughes, in the undefined hope that somehow this would make the company high-tech.

- They build an organization dedicated above all to accomplishing their sharply focused goals—to *getting it done* rather than *following the system*. They play down hierarchy, bureaucracy, and internal politicking, as Nucor's tiny, 21-person headquarters staff bears witness.

- They encourage teamwork while promoting individual responsibility and enterprise, rewarding performance by merit bonuses, which even for Nucor's steelworkers can amount to 200 percent of base pay.

- These companies emphasize the importance of their culture: the values, the way of doing things, the shared outlook that gets them to achieve. Newell has a cadre of avid young managers so stamped with the company's goal and character that they are said to be as "Newellized" as the divisions they run.

- Revolutionary companies like to say they are in partnership with their customers. They make it their business to know their customers so well that they know what the customer wants almost better than the customer knows itself. Most of these companies stress the importance of service, which they recognize can be the crucial difference between them and their competitors.

Although one would have difficulty disagreeing with any of these, our view is that many of the skills just described would tend to make one *operationally* more competent. To gain strategic advantage, our view is that one needs to change the rules of play by developing a different business concept than that being practiced by one's competitors. In other words, play the game to your own rules!

The Japanese Rule Book

One could even take this approach and apply it to the success of Japan over the last 30 years. Lee Iacocca has repeatedly pointed out to us that the Japanese "don't play according to the same rules." And he may be right. Alan Blinder, in a *Business Week* article entitled "There Are Capitalists, Then There Are the Japanese" appearing in the October 8, 1990, issue, has documented some of these differences. "Studying the Japanese economy," he notes, "has led me to a tentative conclusion: that market capitalism, Japanese-style, departs so much from conventional Western economic thought that it deserves to be considered a different system." He goes on to quote a high-level official of Japan's Ministry of International Trade and Industry who remarked: "We did the opposite of what American economists said. We violated all the rules." Some examples: Whereas, in America, the system is geared to serving the needs of consumers, the system in Japan is geared to serving the needs of the producers. In America, the consumer is best served by innovating and holding down costs; in Japan, the producer seeks growth to create employment as an integral part of nation building. Whereas cartels are thought of as being detrimental to healthy competition in America, cartels are encouraged in Japan. Whereas American public companies make many decisions on the basis of short-term profits to enhance shareholder value, in Japan, decisions are rarely made on the basis of short-term results or shareholders' concerns. In America, close buyer-vendor relationships are discouraged; in Japan, it is a fundamental concept of their success at quality improvement. Alan Blinder goes on to illustrate a long list of other Japanese practices that are different from those in America.

In a second study of Japanese business practices conducted by *Fortune* magazine and appearing in the December 9, 1991, issue, still another way of changing the rules of play was detected. This one deals with how the Japanese account for costs in the development of new products (Figure 9-1).

> Like its famed quality philosophy, Japan's cost-management system stands Western practice on its head. For example, American companies developing a new product typically design it first and then calculate the cost. If it's too high, the product goes back to the drawing board—or the company settles for a smaller profit. The Japanese start with a target cost based on the price the market is most likely to accept. Then they direct designers and engineers to meet the target.

The Japanese company that has had the greatest success by setting a new set of rules is Toyota. When Toyota entered the car business, its executives visited Ford's plants several times to study Henry Ford's concept for the mass production of automobiles. They concluded that it would not be in their best interest to play the game in this manner. As a result, they set out to completely reinvent the manufacturing process. This new process has since become known as the Toyota Production System and has not only contributed to Toyota's success, but has since been copied by all Japanese companies and is probably the single most

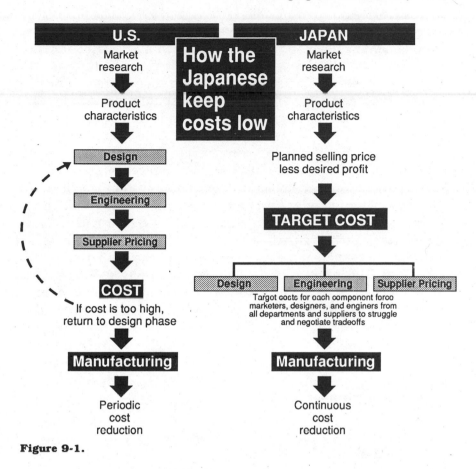

Figure 9-1.

significant factor that has contributed to the dramatic rises we have seen in Japanese quality and productivity since the war.

American industrialists and politicians have spent inordinate amounts of time and effort trying to get the Japanese to play the game according to our rules. Instead they should recognize the fact that maybe—just maybe—the Japanese do not want to play according to our rules. After all, who's been winning the game? A better approach might be to spend time inventing a new game with new rules that are more to our advantage.

There is a blip on the horizon indicating that America may finally be catching on. The field is HDTV (high-definition television). For several years now, a number of so-called experts have been warning that if the U.S. government did not invest billions of dollars in the development of HDTV technology similar to that of the Japanese, America would lose control of the next generation of televisions, and a potentially explosive growth market would revert again to the Japanese. Fortunately, nobody listened because copycatting the Japanese would have been doomed to failure.

Luckily for America, a company called General Instrument decided to change the rules of play and announced a *digital* HDTV! The Japanese system, based on an analog system, consisted of doubling the number of horizontal lines in order to produce better resolution. General Instrument decided that it had to tie its television to a world dominated by digital chips, digital compact disks, and digital telephones. Their system, based on digital technology, will make it easier to manipulate images, enlarge pictures, and even view images from different angles, not to mention what else will be possible as computer and telecommunication technologies continue to converge.

By refusing to play by Japanese rules and by creating new ones and tilting the field to its advantage, one company may lead the way to the United States' reemergence as a powerhouse in the consumer electronics game.

The Moral of the Story

The moral of these examples is this: When you change the rules of play on the leader, you paralyze the leader, sometimes for long periods of time. The reason is simple. The leader's organization is structured to do business according to the rules it has set. Changing that structure is not easy and can sometimes take years. While the leader is immobilized, you can make significant and important gains.

The best way to make these inroads is to conduct your business using tactics that neutralize your competitor's most important strength. Think of ways that *circumvent* the leader's strength. In this manner, you can turn the leader's strength into a vulnerability. Trying to duplicate a competitor's key skill will put you in a race with no end. Run your own race!

This is what we find to be true in all the clients we work with. When everyone in an industry plays the game according to the same rules, no one wins! In other words, there are only marginal changes in market position. Those who make significant gains at a competitors's expense are those who have found a way to tilt the playing field to their advantage by changing the rules of play.

After all, the object of competition is *not* to have an even playing field, but to design a *playing field that is tilted to your advantage,* and to design a playing field that paralyzes the competition. As General Sun Tsu would say, "To subdue the enemy without fighting is the acme of skill."

Again our concepts can be compared to strategies employed by the military. In fact, the very word *strategy* has that connotation built into it. The word comes from the Greek *strategia* and means "a maneuver designed to surprise the enemy."

The same concept applies to business. Do not play the game according to your competitor's rules. *Surprise* the enemy by changing the rules of play! If you are constantly being "surprised" by the enemy, this is a clear signal of a defensive, reactive strategy. Change it. A proactive strategy is one that is constantly surprising the enemy and keeping the competitor in a defensive position!

To quote General Sun Tsu once more, "All warfare is based on deception."

10

The Future of Strategic Success: Market Fragmentation versus Market Segmentation

Although corporate executives would claim that they are constantly bombarded by changes that affect their business, in reality there are very few macro changes that have significant impact on corporations. If a CEO fails to recognize these macro trends, it could mean corporate death. However, the CEO who does detect a macro change early in its evolution and constructs a strategy to capitalize on it can reap substantial reward.

Two such macro trends are currently at work today. One is a demographic change—the aging population of most Western countries—which will affect every company in the world for the next 25 years. The other, and the one I wish to concentrate on in this chapter, has already occurred but has been missed by most corporate CEOs, particularly in the United States.

The most significant change of the last 15 years is that the majority of the economies of the Western world have gone from "push" economies to "pull" economies.

"What's the difference?" you may ask.

"Very substantial," I would answer.

Push to Pull Economy

In a "push" economy there is more demand than supply and the *producer* reigns (Figure 10-1). From 1945 to the mid-1970s such was the case in the West. Most companies, particularly U.S. ones, were riding this wave. Everything they produced was immediately gobbled up by long lines of customers craving their products. One only needs to go back to the introduction of television in the mid-1950s to understand this phenomenon. If you were around back then, you will remember how the entire neighborhood would gather at the window of the local appliance store to watch the TV set through the store window. The next morning, there was always a long line of customers waiting to purchase their first TV. It didn't matter much to the customer that resolution was poor and that the picture kept rotating on the screen; the goal was to get a set before the store sold out—more demand than supply. This situation lasted until the mid-1970s.

Today, the opposite situation exists. With the advent of Japanese, Korean, Singaporean, Taiwanese, and European products, there is more supply than demand. As a result, the rules of the game have changed significantly. In a "pull" economy, the *customer* reigns. Unfortunately, few CEOs have noticed.

Market Fragmentation versus Segmentation

How does one deal with a push versus a pull economy? In a push economy, the producer controls the market and the key to success is market segmentation. This is the concept of grouping large numbers of customers with *similar* needs together and providing them with a generic product. It's the Henry Ford approach to

ECONOMY

PUSH	PULL
⇧ DEMAND VS. SUPPLY	⇧ SUPPLY VS. DEMAND
PRODUCER ⇉	CUSTOMER ⇉
MARKET SEGMENTATION	MARKET FRAGMENTATION
LARGE # CUSTOMERS SIMILAR NEEDS	SMALLER # CUSTOMERS DISSIMILAR NEEDS
GENERIC PRODUCT	TAILORED PRODUCT
COMMODITY PRICES	PREMIUM PRICES
LONG PRODUCTION RUNS	SHORTER PRODUCTION RUNS
EFFICIENT MANUFACTURING	FLEXIBILE, EFFECTIVE MANUFACTURING
LONG PRODUCT CYCLES	SHORTER PRODUCT CYCLES
STRONG BRAND LOYALTY	LITTLE BRAND LOYALTY
PRODUCT INNOVATION	PROCESS INNOVATION
FIXED RULES	CHANGING RULES
STURDY AND STABLE	FAST AND NIMBLE

Figure 10-1. (*Copyright © 1991 by Decision Processes International. All rights reserved.*)

business. "You can have any color car you want as long as it's black." This has been the approach followed by all U.S. producers since the end of World War II. But unfortunately, it does not work in a pull economy. A company must practice the opposite concept of *market fragmentation* to be successful.

Market fragmentation is the opposite concept of identifying smaller groups of customers with *dissimilar* needs and responding with *customized* products. The world's most successful companies today are practicing market fragmentation. Companies in trouble are still clinging to the outdated market segmentation. Again, a variety of examples exist.

In the automobile industry, which was probably the first to go from push to pull, one of the most successful companies is Toyota. The reason is simple. Toyota has so mastered its business and manufacturing processes that a customer can enter a dealer's office in Japan on Monday morning, configure the car he or she wants, and take delivery of it on Friday afternoon—custom-made to the buyer's specifications. Toyota expects to bring this concept to the United States in 1993.

Even BMW, the German automaker, attributes its current success to market fragmentation. As *Business Week* reported in a 1991 article entitled "`Grill to Grill' with Japan":

> In Europe, where BMW gets 75% of its sales, most cars are made to order. That's why BMW offers a big à la carte menu of models, engines, colors, and options. "Each customer can have a unique car," says Eberhard von Kuenheim (CEO). Japanese competitors offer far fewer choices. He complains: "They are building 100, 200, even 400 exactly identical cars a day."

I hate to think what he would say about the American manufacturers.

Sony markets a different version of its Walkman in Norway than it does in Sweden, two of its smallest worldwide markets. Why? Sony discovered that these two areas had unique needs that required a slightly different product.

Twenty months after 3M introduced its unique Post-it™ Notes, the company had developed more than 100 versions of the original product to cater to a variety of slightly different needs in the marketplace. No other competitor was able to keep up with such a pace of product proliferation.

Castrol, the oil lubricant specialist, has no oil reserves nor does it own any refineries or service stations. What Castrol does have, however, is over 3000 different formulas of lubricants, each tailored to a specific application. While the major oil companies try to satisfy the market with one or two generic lubricants, Castrol can provide a specific formula especially conceived to fulfill the requirements of each customer's specific application.

FLEXcon, a client based in Spencer, Massachusetts, has a similar approach. Whereas the giant chemical companies provide multipurpose, generic adhesives to printers who produce printed packaging material, FLEXcon develops a special formula for each printer. FLEXcon's ability to tailor a solution to meet each printer's specific need represents that companies competitive advantage.

In the retailing business, Sears is suffering from a double whammy. On one hand, a number of specialty retailers are fragmenting the market away from Sears. Sears' strategy of being all things to all people—as reflected by the broad array of merchandise, from furniture to financial services—is being decimated by a new brand of retailers such as The Limited and The Gap, each catering to a much narrower range of needs. On the other hand, a couple of players such as Wal-Mart and Home Depot are changing the rules of play. Don't buy shares in Sears for a number of years to come.

Even McDonald's is feeling the pinch of market fragmentation. A host of smaller, more nimble competitors are forcing McDonald's to rethink its entire strategy. Companies such as Chili's, Taco Bell, Olive Garden, and others are dividing and conquering what was once a large, homogeneous market for hamburgers.

In the mundane world of pens, pencils, and markers, the Sanford Company of Illinois produces a return on equity of 24 percent and sales increases of 14 percent per year. How? By fragmenting the market to pieces. Sanford keeps broadening the market by niching it to death. Sanford has markers for all types of applications, from marking clothes in laundrymarts to nonsmearing markers for use on fax paper. In between, it has watercolor markers for toddlers of every age and talent. Again, the myth of the mature market has been proven to be false. As *Forbes* observed in the August 5, 1991, issue about this company: "As the fountain pen was dying 40 years ago, few would have thought Sanford would survive into the 1990s. Fewer still would have predicted that the market would price it like a growth stock. Impressive job, Hank Pearsall."

There are many ramifications of the market fragmentation versus segmentation approach, and the remainder of this chapter will explore these.

Differentiated versus Commodity Products

One of the first impacts of market fragmentation is that it almost makes commodity products and their providers obsolete. Because the practitioners of market segmentation respond with generic products that attempt to satisfy large groups of users, these products are usually easily duplicatable and, before long, become "commodity" items. Market fragmentation, on the other hand, results in a wide variety of custom-made products, each differentiated to solve a unique set of requirements. Because customer needs are always evolving, so too are the products. This makes it more difficult for competitors to emulate.

In fact, the companies and industries that are struggling today are the ones that have not adjusted to market fragmentation and are losing ground to the those that are practicing this concept. The strategy of the "fragmentor" is to identify large, commodity markets and to fragment them into smaller pieces to the fragmentor's advantage.

In the media industry, CBS, ABC, and NBC are going through this trauma. The industry is being fragmented by the cable providers who, in turn, are fragmenting programming to address the more specific needs of smaller segments of the audience. Thus, the remarkable growth and success of MTV, A&E, ESPN, and others.

Ted Turner is running ahead of the pack. Not only has he changed the rules of play with his worldwide news network

CNN, but he is also practicing market fragmentation through cable television. In addition to his news network, Turner has introduced an all-movie channel for movie buffs, an all-sports network for sports buffs, and soon to be introduced—an all-cartoon network for cartoon buffs.

Bill Ziff of Ziff Communications and Dale Lang of Lang Communications are doing the same thing to the barons of the print media. For several decades the goal of magazine publishers was to publish a magazine that could find an audience of 7 to 10 million readers. Several did at one time and became known as the "seven sisters." These included *McCall's, Redbook,* and *Good Housekeeping.* Lang and Ziff have done exactly the opposite. Lang is the publisher of a number of women's magazines, each tailored to a unique set of feminine needs. One, for example, is called *Working Woman* and another is called *Working Mother.* Each has a subscriber base of only a million readers, but the magazines are highly successful. In fact, *Working Woman* has been the most successful of any magazine launched in the last decade.

Ziff, on the other hand, can be considered the founder of "special interest" magazines. He started such titles as *Car and Driver, Yachting, PC Magazine, MacUser,* and *Computer Shopper.* Ziff clearly detected the shift from market segmentation, as being practiced by the seven sister–types, to market fragmentation. As he said to *Forbes* in an interview in the June 10, 1991, issue: "When I started in this business, mass magazines were dominant. Today we live in an age of stratified, separated, targeted markets that are information-hungry. The future of all advertising-supported media is *narrow casting,* not broadcasting."

Hallmark once dominated the market for greeting cards. Today, 70 percent of the market has been fragmented by a dozen or so smaller companies who offer a card for just about any occasion, including no occasion.

In the 1970s, Adolph Coors, the brewing company, was in dire straits. Its growth had stopped and so had its profits. In the 1980s, Coors discovered market fragmentation. When the "light" beer craze arrived, both Miller and Anheuser-Busch introduced one brand and tried to capture the largest share of the market. Coors, on the other hand, introduced three different brands, each tailored to a different set of customers. One in particular called the Silver Bullet was geared especially to women. As a result, Coors doubled its sales in the 1980s and has edged its way up to number 3 next to Busch and Miller. Coors' objective is to displace Miller as number 2 by the end of this decade by more fragmentation.

Another example is IBM. IBM's strategy has long been to satisfy the largest number of customers with standard, generic products. Thus the success of its model 360. Fortunately for IBM, there were no other suppliers that the customer could turn to. As one large, ex-IBM customer said to this author: "IBM told us what we needed; they did not listen to what we thought we needed." With the advent of other mainframe suppliers and the PC, even IBM is now eating humble pie. Compaq, Apple, Sun, AST, and several others are fragmenting the market while IBM is still practicing segmentation.

Premium Price versus Low Price

One of the disadvantages of the market segmentation approach is that it leads to generic products, as already mentioned, and to generic prices. Because all products are very similar, so are the prices. And most transactions have a tendency to drift to the level of "low price wins" because customers see no difference in one product compared to another.

The advantage of market fragmentation is often the opposite. Products have been tailored to very specific needs, so the "solution" is usually different than the generic product, and "added value" can be perceived by each customer. This allows for premium pricing, and each transaction is concluded on the basis of value instead of price. Higher margins are therefore possible.

Both Lang and Ziff get premium prices for their publications compared to the publishers of the "seven sisters." The reason is simple. Their magazines deliver a much more narrow, but more targeted audience with differentiated needs. The same is true at FLEXcon.

Short Runs versus
Long Runs

A great advantage of market segmentation is that it provides the producer with long manufacturing runs that enable it to attain maximum production efficiencies and, thus, profits. Unfortunately, the opposite is again the case in market fragmentation. Manufacturing versatility, not efficiency, is the key skill in this new mode. Again, U.S. companies have been slow to notice this change. As Michael Dertouzos, Director of MIT's Laboratory for Computer Science, has pointed out in an article in the Nov./Dec. 1990 issue of *Chief Executive:*

> U.S. industry clings to outmoded strategies, like inflexible mass production of a large number of standard goods that does not reflect the growing demand for individualized custom quality products. This system, pioneered by Henry Ford, can be likened to a gigantic wheel of production, where workers, suppliers, and other participants are highly specialized cogs. The objective is to keep the wheel turning, no matter what. Anyone who misbehaves is replaced. By contrast, the new systems of production, both in the best-practice U.S. companies and abroad, entail a nimbler approach where broadly trained workers produce shorter runs of tailored goods. They are winning over the older system of mass production.

An industry currently undergoing the trials and tribulations of the transitions from a push to pull mode is that of textiles. In the United States, textile manufacturers have concentrated on materials that can be produced in large quantities such as denim and sheeting. The problem they face, however, is that the retailers that are winning today are those that are fragmenting the market with a host of styles and fashions that require a much wider variety of materials and finishes, but in smaller quantities. These are retailers such as The Limited and The Gap. Both these companies are going offshore to satisfy their requirements, not because these manufacturers are less costly but rather, because they are more flexible. As Lesly Wexler, CEO of The Limited, told *Business Week* in an interview appearing in the February 3, 1992, issue: "The problem with U.S. textile mills is that they don't make what we want to buy" In a pull economy, the customer is king!

Production Efficiency versus Production Versatility

Under a system that stresses long production runs and commodity products that can easily be duplicated by competitors, the key to winning is by striving to become the low cost producer. The concept of market fragmentation, however, focuses on production versatility—in other words, the ability to change from one product to another on the same line without losing efficiency.

In Germany, Heinz Grieffenberger took over an ailing company in 1983 called ABM Baumiller, a maker of motors and gearboxes for cranes. What he found was a company making a few standard products for a large number of customers. He quickly replaced the entire production process in order to tailor his products to individual customer's needs. "I can switch production to a different product within seconds," he boasted to *Business Week,* as reported in a February 3, 1992, article.

To be successful in the future, companies will have to learn to make their production processes as versatile as Toyota's without losing efficiency. FLEXcon, for example, prides itself on its ability to "tweak" its highly complex volume-intensive coating process to supply custom-tailored orders of 200 yards when all other competitors demand 10 times the quantity for a minimum order. And FLEXcon has mastered this versatility without losing efficiency.

In the computer peripheral business, a rising star is Exabyte Corporation, which has developed an ingenious device that can increase the amount of information stored on computer disks. The company, started in 1987, has already grown from nothing to $170 million. Although the company's growth was based on an exclusive technology that gave it a monopoly in the marketplace, market fragmentation was at the root of its success. Its CEO, Peter Behrendt, said in an interview with *Planning Forum:* "Our customers wanted the product `customized.' We had to set up a product in 100 different flavors; set up a manufacturing system rather than batching things, that at the end of the line produces the one the customer wants. We solved that problem."

Dell Computers is another example of a company that has

changed the rules of marketing PCs not so much through the use of direct marketing methods but by practicing market fragmentation. It has achieved the ability to customize every PC ordered to each customer's individual needs by transforming its assembly process into one of the most flexible in the industry. Dell has simplified its product and component configurations into a "made-to-order" manufacturing operation by pushing customization to the end of production and transmitting order information to the shop floor every 24 hours. This has resulted to three-to-four-day production and delivery cycles.

Product versus Process Innovation

Under a push economy, when there is always a long line of waiting customers for your product, the type of innovation needed is usually that of product innovation. This is so because there are few competitors and the occasional introduction of new product versions is enough to succeed.

In a pull economy, however, with multiple competitors, product innovation alone is not sufficient to succeed. Process innovation is now a required skill. Historically, the United States has not been very capable at process innovation compared to the Japanese and the Germans. And the reason can be found by looking at where each country's R&D money has been invested over the last 30 years.

	Product R&D (percent)	Process R&D (percent)
United States	70	30
Japan	30	70
Germany	50	50

Germany's balanced expenditure between product and process innovation probably explains why it has been even more successful than the Japanese since the end of World War II.

Lower Brand Loyalty

Another major effect of the pull economy and a contributor to the success of companies practicing market fragmentation is the change in the loyalty of consumers to traditional brands.

In a push economy, there is strong brand loyalty because there is restriction of choice for the consumer and limited supply. As a result, the producer talks itself into believing that its products have strong brand following. In a pull economy, brand loyalty suffers and, faced with more choices of ever increasing quality, the consumer's loyalty is to himself or herself and not the producer.

A result of this shift is the current cry among advertising agencies for higher advertising budgets to regain brand loyalty. The trend will continue to be in the opposite direction. A major winner in this shift from diminishing brand loyalty will be the providers of private label brands whose sales have been on the upswing for several years at the expense of the traditional brands.

Changing Rules versus Fixed Rules

Under a push economy, the rules of play are set by the producer and forced onto customers. As long as a push economy exists, the producer enforces those rules and thrives from them. Under a pull economy, not only are the rules set by the customer but they are constantly changing. As a result, market fragmentators are very nimble people constantly monitoring and adapting to the evolution of customer needs in order to find new opportunities to identify slightly different needs that will lead to slightly different products which will allow them to fragment the market even further and make it still more difficult for their competitors.

Once, as I was walking through one of Caterpillar's plants, I noticed a red tractor in one corner and a blue tractor in another. "Are those competitor tractors that you plan to strip down?" I asked. "No. They're ours," replied the vice president. "Some customers don't always want yellow."

Ten years ago this would have been heresy at Caterpillar. This company could do no wrong from 1925 to 1982. But then, in 1982, even mighty Caterpillar was hit by the pull economy. Fortunately, Caterpillar has recognized the change and is responding. Today, Caterpillar is customizing 70 percent of its machines to the needs of each individual customer.

As reported in the June 1989 issue of *EuroBusiness*, the CEO of Matsushita has said, "In the future the mass market will be the individual." A company that already practices this concept is the Karsten Company in Phoenix. It has taken a substantial share of the golf club equipment market by applying the same principle of fragmentation. Whereas most companies create generic clubs to fit all sizes of players, Karsten customizes each set to each player's physical dimensions. As its advertisements state:

> We at Karsten have always designed and built PING golf clubs to each customer's individual specifications. Just send us your golf size, height and fingertip-to-floor measurements. These measurements help us make certain that the lie of each club rests properly on the ground. The lie of each iron must also be in proper relation to the length of the shaft. This is why a golfer's height is taken into consideration.

When was the last time you were asked these questions when you bought a set of golf clubs?

Companies that do not learn to practice market fragmentation, even to the level of single customers, will be the dinosaurs of this decade.

The Myth of Mature Markets

Some people would claim that the reason products become generic, prices come down to the lowest level, and growth stops is that the "market is mature." Mature markets, in our view, are a myth.

Consider some examples. Who would have thought 10 years ago that people would pay $300 for a pair of shoes? Running shoes at that! After all, everyone had a pair and the market was "mature." Then along came Nike and Reebok!

Who would have thought 10 years ago that people would be paying $3000 for a bicycle. After all, everyone had one and the market was "mature." Then along came Shimano and its "mountain" bikes with 21 speeds!

In yet another business, the former management of A. E. Staley thought that the corn milling business was "mature" and decided to embark on a diversification spree to become a consumer products marketer that nearly destroyed the company. Its new owners, Tate & Lyle, decided to rededicate the company to its previous core business with great success. Its CEO, Neil Shaw, told *Forbes* in an interview appearing in the June 24, 1991, issue, "The old management took their eyes off the ball. We got back to doing what we do best—we're corn millers." With its old strategy back in vogue, Staley introduced new products, one of which is a fat substitute made from corn that has reversed the firm's financial performance overnight and put it back on a highly profitable road.

As mentioned previously, Adolph Coors has managed to grow impressively in the beer business—an industry considered by Busch and Miller to be "mature."

Even in the liquor industry, probably one of the world's most mature industries, that concept is a myth—not decided by us, but by the CEO of one of the industry's most successful players. In a market where consumption is dropping 1 percent per year on a worldwide basis, the CEO of Guinness argues, as reported in the November 4, 1991, issue of *Fortune:* "Consumption is not actually a very good indicator in any business of whether there are any opportunities there." To prove his point, CEO Anthony Tennant defers to his company's performance in 1991—$1.2 billion of earnings on sales of $3.8 billion for an operating profit margin of 31 percent. Furthermore, all four of the major players in this field produced margins of over 25 percent. So much for mature markets.

The concept of a "mature market," in our view, resides in the mind of the beholder. In other words, it is a state of mind. Management convinces itself that its business is "mature" and, as a result, two things start to happen.

First, the company stops looking for opportunities because it has convinced itself there are no more. Therefore, it stops innovating. Second, it starts diverting its resources to unrelated opportunities that take it way off course, usually with disastrous results.

There are always opportunities, particularly if one is practicing market fragmentation! As the CEO of Pepsico, a company that is viewed as being in a "mature" industry but is outpacing its competitors in growth, puts it in a March 1991 *Fortune* article: "If the market you're in isn't growing, you'd better find a way to make it grow."

11
The Dos and Don'ts of Strategic Alliances

The buzz phrase heard most frequently throughout the corporate world today is *strategic alliance.* All the management gurus are on the bandwagon espousing the need to form strategic alliances in order to survive and prosper in the future. The concept is simple enough—if you can't fight them, join them. In other words, it's easier to form an alliance with a competitor than to fight that competitor.

Many of these alliances will fail, we believe, because they are being formed for the wrong reasons. In the first place, I must admit that I do not favor alliances. Alliances generally reduce competition, and reduced competition is not good for the consumer or the companies involved. Alliances usually produce higher prices for the consumer and breed complacency in the joined companies.

However, if you feel your company must enter into such a venture, here are some dos and don'ts drawn from years of experience from our strategy consulting work.

Don'ts

Don't Form an Alliance to Correct a Weakness

Many companies form alliances to correct a weakness they possess. This is not a good start. The reason is simple. The party that brings a weakness to the alliance will be, from that day forward, at the mercy of the other partner and subservient to that other party. Even though the alliance may be 50-50, the weak partner will never be an equal partner because weaknesses don't bring leverage in the marketplace.

A good example is General Motors' current alliance with Toyota in a joint manufacturing plant in Freemont, California. GM went into the venture to correct a weakness—its inability to manufacture high-quality small cars. GM thought it could acquire that know-how from Toyota through an alliance. Ten years later, GM still doesn't know how to make a good-quality small car. In fact, the car that bears the Toyota nameplate from the plant outsells the GM version 6 to 1.

Another example, also from the automobile industry, is the Honda-Rover alliance in the United Kingdom. Rover's objective in this alliance was to correct a weakness—a lack of innovative car designs. It thought that by coproducing a Honda model it would protect its European share and help it penetrate the U.S. market. Neither of these two goals has materialized. Rover became so dependent on Honda that Rover has had no benefit at all. Honda has derived all the benefit. Not only did the alliance give Honda an entry into Europe (140,000 cars in 1990), Honda is now increasing its capacity to 300,000 cars. Rover's capacity has dwindled to less than 30,000.

Don't Form an Alliance with a Partner That Is Trying to Correct a Weakness of Its Own

The rationale, again, is simple. Your company will inherit that weakness! You may end up worse off than you were before if you become the dominant partner in the alliance. The worst of all worlds is an alliance of two partners, each of which is trying to correct a weakness. This type of marriage is doomed to failure from the start.

In the last few years there have been many alliances and mergers in the financial services industry. Unfortunately, many have been for the wrong reasons. A good example is the 1987 merger of Dallas-based Interfirst with RepublicBank. The new company, First RepublicBank Corporation, collapsed because both banks had brought to the table an overwhelming load of bad real estate loans. As *Business Week* noted, in an article "Handicapping the Bank Merger Game!" in the March 22, 1991, issue, at the time: "In this instance, two weak banks sought security in each other's arms only to find they had created a bigger but weaker bank."

A second example comes from Germany where two steel makers, Krupp and Hoesch are talking merger. "This is a marriage of weakness" says Barclays' de Zoete Wedd. Not a good basis to start a marriage. One can almost predict the eventual worse position of these two partners.

Two plus two sometimes equals three!

Never, Never License Proprietary Technology

One only needs to look at what has happened to the United States over the last 25 years to understand this rule. Sony acquired its transistor technology from Bell Laboratories for $25,000. A few years later, there were no more manufacturers of radios in the United States. Sony also acquired its videotape know-how from Ampex. In the United States, Ampex is no longer in the business. Unless you have very tight control of its use, licensing proprietary technology will always come back to haunt you!

In the article "Use a Long Spoon" (*Forbes*, 1986), C. K. Prahalad, of the University of Michigan, made a study of eight such alliances and concluded that Western companies had too easily given up control of key technologies to the Japanese. Prahalad suggests that Western companies should think of these deals not as "strategic alliances" but as "competitive collaboration." He explains, "That would alert the organization to what they should protect." He also suggests, "Don't let your partner *underwork your core technology and skills.*" If you do so, "Japanese companies will build an ever more complex *competency* base and Western companies will surrender ever more control over their own competitiveness."

We would certainly agree with Prahalad. While working with owner-managed companies, we have noticed that these companies *never* license their *key skills* or *expertise* to anyone. Much more than publicly run companies, the CEO strategist in these organizations has a very clear understanding as to what area of the business drives the organization's strategy and what areas of excellence make that strategy work. And control over this strategic weapon is never relinquished!

Many U.S. multinationals are currently losing sight of that notion. The latest fad is to embark on "strategic alliances" with Japanese companies in an attempt to improve U.S. competitiveness. Unfortunately, these U.S. companies are losing sight of their driving force and are entering into alliances where they are giving up control of their strategic weapon.

Don't Form Alliances around Products or Markets

Most alliances fail because companies form alliances in order to exploit the similarity of certain products or markets. This rarely works. As proof one only needs to review the multitude of broken alliances between companies that have attempted this.

Dos

Rule 1: Form an Alliance to Exploit a Unique Strength

When forming an alliance, bring to the table a strength that you possess that is *unique* to you. In other words, no other competitor has this unique characteristic. The rationale? Only unique strengths can be sustained and defended over time. Even relative strengths—those that you have to a greater extent than a competitor but share with that competitor—are not the best upon which to build a successful alliance. Relative strengths can be acquired or duplicated but cannot be sustained over time.

Rule 2: Form an Alliance with a Partner That Has a Unique Strength of Its Own

A marriage of unique strengths is the ideal. Looking to build a relationship by combining the synergy of strengths that are unique to each partner represents a venture with the highest probability of success.

Rule 3: Form an Alliance When Neither Partner Has the Ability nor the Desire to Acquire the Other Party's Unique Strength

This is the key rule of successful alliances. If one of the parties has the intention of acquiring the other partner's unique strength, there will be no trust in the relationship from the beginning!

A good example of one such successful alliance is 3M's venture with Squibb. 3M brings some polymer chemistry technology that can be applied to the development of drugs that Squibb cannot duplicate, and Squibb brings a distribution system to doctors and drugstores that 3M has no intention of replicating.

Corning is a premier example of a company that has engineered a series of successful alliances over the last few decades. The formula it has followed is the one just described. To each alliance, Corning brings its unique strength—its technology—and then seeks a partner that has a unique strength of its own. The other party is not usually in a position to duplicate Corning's technology, and Corning does not intend to acquire or duplicate the other party's unique contribution to the venture. The result? A string of successful ventures.

At Corning, alliances are an integral part of its strategy and its culture and not something out of the mainstream of business, which is usually the case in most other companies.

Two more recent alliances may prove to be winning combinations. The first is Bristol-Myers' merger with Squibb. Squibb's strength lies in its ability to develop and market ethical drugs, whereas Bristol-Myers' strength is in over-the-counter, nonprescription drugs. The combination of these two firms' research budget might just prove that sometimes two plus two equals five!

The second is Apple's alliance with IBM. Although many experts are skeptical, this alliance could possibly revolutionize the computer industry and be good for both companies. The reason: Both are bringing a uniqueness that the other party will find difficult to duplicate. Apple brings its vaunted and unique graphic and user-friendly software while IBM brings its powerful RS6000 computer chip. This alliance could result in a quantum leap development of a new generation of PCs and work stations and could be a major threat to other competitors such as Sun and Compaq.

Rule 4: Form Alliances around Capabilities

Rather than seek a marriage around products and markets, it is much wiser to form alliances around unique skills, capabilities, know-how, or technologies. Let the alliance develop products and markets later. The probability of success will increase many times.

Profit Is No Replacement for Strategic Fit

Sometimes an alliance might even turn out to be extremely profitable, but still these don't necessarily represent sound strategic fits. R. J. Reynolds, the cigarette giant, once had that experience. In an era when diversification was a corporate craze, Reynolds purchased Aminoil, an oil exploration firm, and Sea-Land Industries, an ocean shipper. Although both purchases turned out to be extremely profitable for Reynolds, the company decided to sell these investments. T. J. Wilson, Reynolds' ex-CEO, explained to *Business Week* (June 6, 1984) that Reynolds was "consumer-driven" and did not understand these two businesses nor could it transfer the expertise it had to these industries. "A marketing orientation is the common thread running through our business," said Wilson. As a result, Wilson decided to return to "consumer-driven" businesses where Reynolds' area of excellence—marketing skills—can be applied even though these businesses may be more competitive. Wilson obviously felt that Reynolds' marketing excellence is the edge that the company brings to the market. Lesson: Diversification is not necessarily good for everyone, and profit alone should not be the driving force!

12

CEOs Talk about the Strategic Thinking Process

This chapter is a series of interviews that were conducted with the CEOs of several of our client organizations. Each CEO talks about the situation his organization was facing and how the concepts and process described in the previous chapters helped in their efforts to formulate, articulate, and change the direction of their respective companies.

George Schaefer, Ex-CEO and Director, Caterpillar Inc.

These days no one can afford sacred cows.

Caterpillar has undergone more change in the last decade than at any other time in its history. In many respects, our experiences parallel those of the entire U.S. manufacturing sector. We enjoyed decades of uninterrupted growth and prosperity, then got hit hard in the early 1980s by a worldwide recession and tough foreign competition. We moved into the survival mode in the short term, then set out to develop a long-term strategy that would make us a stronger global competitor. Let me offer some insight into what we've been through at Caterpillar, and in so doing, attempt to give some additional perspective on strategic change in the manufacturing sector of the economy.

We are best known for our big yellow bulldozers, but we sell a complete line of construction machines, lift trucks, and engines—a line that numbers approximately 300 models. We are also involved in a variety of ancillary businesses: financing, venture capital, logistics, insurance, and global countertrade, to name just a few. We have our headquarters in Peoria, Illinois, but our plants are based all over the world. Our products are sold and supported through an independent dealer organization more than 200 members strong. Our history is not unlike the history of other U.S.-based manufacturers. We incorporated in the 1920s, rode out the depression of the 1930s, picked up steam in the 1940s, then grew rapidly through the fifties, sixties, and seventies.

From the 1940s onward, each decade brought new opportunities for growth. First came sales to the military during World War II. Then postwar infrastructure development in Europe and Japan followed by the massive U.S. interstate highway program, large infrastructure projects in South America, and a fourfold increase in oil prices—which led to an explosion in demand for all products related to energy exploration. Year after year, we cranked up production—building new facilities and increasing capacity. But it was never enough. We simply couldn't grow fast enough to fill all the orders.

As for our competitors—I won't go so far as to say we didn't have any, but the fact is, we were the undisputed leader worldwide. In the United States we competed against a handful of American companies. Together we supplied 85 to 95 percent of the construction equipment sold here. Outside the United States we were, in effect, the only global competitor, selling against a host of national companies. Each country had its own key players, few of which ever sold outside their borders.

By the 1970s, however, with business booming in the United

States and places like South America and the Middle East, some overseas competitors—particularly the Japanese—began venturing into the world marketplace. Over the years they had quietly made steady gains in quality and productivity. Now they were ready to challenge us for the business.

So, as the 1980s unfolded, the competitive environment was beginning to change. But we were still ahead of the pack and still earning record sales and profit.

Then, like Napoleon, we met our Waterloo. Our market collapsed. Fifty years of uninterrupted growth came to a screeching halt in 1982 when the world entered a recession, oil prices plummeted, and South American countries began reneging on their loans. Almost overnight demand dried up, and our industry was awash with capacity. Some estimate that supply exceeded demand by as much as 40 percent.

To aggravate the situation, the U.S. dollar soared to record heights against the yen, giving our Japanese competitors a tremendous cost advantage. There wasn't a lot of business out there, but anybody who was in the market for a new machine was looking carefully at the bottom line. And because Japanese manufacturers were pricing their products as much as 40 percent below ours, we were forced to discount heavily or lose the business.

We battled for the business and did what we had to do to preserve market share. In the final analysis, we lost about a billion dollars over a three-year period. It was a humbling experience. Our long years of success had made us complacent, even arrogant, and few among us were prepared to accept the fact that our world had changed—permanently.

We were slow to react, but in time we were forced to take action to survive. We made a series of defensive moves to help stop the bleeding. Nine plants were closed. Employment was reduced by more than 30,000. We cut salaries, began purchasing more parts and components from lower cost suppliers, deferred capital spending, and so on. These actions allowed us to reduce costs by about 20 percent between 1982 and 1986.

During that time we also launched a number of longer-term initiatives aimed at strengthening our competitive position. We doubled the size of our product line so that we could serve a larger customer base, and branched off into new businesses outside, but closely related to, our traditional business. The most costly endeavor we undertook was a factory modernization program, a $1.5 billion investment designed to improve the competitiveness of our worldwide manufacturing base.

These are all major commitments to our future. They'll pay off in the long run, but in the meantime, they're draining profitability and making some people on Wall Street nervous. It must be admitted, we do share the Street's dissatisfaction with current earnings, but we don't share its preoccupation with short-term results. Our commitment to the long term is unwavering. It has to be, given the strength and tenacity of our competitors.

Although these short- and long-term initiatives will improve Caterpillar's competitive position, it became clear to us early on that they would not be enough. We determined, therefore, that in order to sustain an advantage over very aggressive competitors, we would have to develop an explicit and fully integrated business strategy—and communicate it clearly to all members of our organization. The top people in the company have spent the last two years hammering out that strategy, with a great deal of assistance from a small group of senior managers known around Caterpillar as the Strategic Planning Committee, or the SPC for short. The SPC is a cross section of Caterpillar managers, with expertise ranging from research to computer integration to marketing to parts distribution. The one thing all committee members have in common is a willingness to challenge traditional thinking: There isn't a "yes man" in the bunch.

We began by assessing the external environment, identifying key trends in our industry and projecting how the business would change between now and the year 2000.

We also gained the perspective of other major companies that had successfully undergone change. Top executives from Digital, USX, Ford, Hewlett-Packard, and other organizations gave us a better understanding of the risks and rewards associated with strategic change.

We organized a whole host of things to assess our competitive position, including a comprehensive evaluation of our strengths and weaknesses, lengthy studies of our most formidable competitors, and a complete market segmentation analysis. Eventually, we reached the stage where we had done enough studying. It was time to articulate a strategy. To do so, we employed the Strategic Thinking Process developed by Michel Robert of Decision Processes International.

This process provides a framework, a road map, through which a management team such as ours can rationally evaluate a wide variety of inputs and come out with a strategy that makes sense to all of us.

We have worked with several top consultants, each contributing to varying degrees. But we were still floundering, despite help from some of the top consultants available. We simply had too much good advice. The DPI process helped us sort everything out, to better utilize the inputs of all the others. Through the process we were able, as a group, to build a strategy we all understand clearly and agree on. There is a tendency to debate strategic thinking *ad infinitum*. The DPI approach forced us through to a conclusion.

We developed a strategy statement and vision for the company. As you can imagine, achieving consensus on these two documents was no small task. But after some vexatious arguments, we eventually reached agreement, and both documents were distributed to employees worldwide so that they all could understand just what kind of company we intended to become.

Once we had a firm grasp on where we wanted to take the company, we identified the critical issues that had the potential to prevent us from achieving our mission and becoming the company we envision. Those issues were discussed in depth at a week-long meeting of about 75 key managers. Now the organization has been challenged to resolve them. To ensure that we do indeed overcome the obstacles that stand in the way of our success, each critical issue has been assigned to an officer of the company who will be held accountable for its resolution.

Accountability is one of the principal characteristics we are striving to build into our organization as we restructure to support the strategic plan. The Strategic Planning Committee will remain in full force on an ongoing basis, utilizing the DPI process as a catalyst. Specific business plans will be reviewed within its context.

Caterpillar announced its intention to restructure in January 1991. The basic framework is in place now. It is flatter and more flexible than our current organization. We've divided the company into 17 autonomous divisions: 13 profit centers and 4 service groups.

The goal is to become more responsive to the needs of our diverse customer base. We will bring together the various functional areas—design, manufacturing, marketing—and hold the team accountable for profitably serving a specific customer group. They will set their own targets, develop their own work plans, make their own decisions, and be rewarded on the basis of individual and group performance.

Today the organization is by no means complete. We are still busy refining it with help from the people who'll have to make it work. We expect the process to be largely complete by mid-year [1991]. Then the real work begins: fostering and accelerating the cultural change that has to accompany the organizational change.

This entire phase of strategic change—forming the planning committee, working our way through the process, crafting the mission and vision, and reshaping the organization—has taken about two-and-a-half years. It is our belief that the strategy we're making to our product line and manufacturing facilities will allow us to achieve and sustain a long-term competitive advantage.

As my direct involvement in Caterpillar's strategic planning effort comes to a close, I think back on some of the things we learned; from our external advisers, from the executives we interviewed, and from one another, as we made our way through this laborious process. Several key points were driven home to us over and over throughout the course of our work. None of the concepts was particularly earthshaking. Most were fairly simple. But in spite of their simplicity, their value to Caterpillar cannot be underestimated.

First, an explicit strategy is absolutely essential. Implicit is not good enough in the competitive environment in which we operate today.

Second, we have to be willing to question everything from an external perspective. These days, no one can afford sacred cows. If some aspect of the business is not performing, have the courage to get rid of it.

Third, ongoing competitive analysis is critical. Know all you can legally know about your competitors, and establish a formal system to do just that.

Fourth, on diversification: As you explore new opportunities for growth, stay close to your core business and maintain leadership within it. Be open to change, but diversify with great care. There are many horror stories about companies that have diversified into completely unrelated fields. Stick to what you do best and you'll greatly improve the odds for successful diversification.

Fifth, on the usefulness of a separate strategic planning group: A small corporate planning team can be effective in providing strategic direction, but basic strategies must come from the operating units. Be sure to keep the corporate planning team focused on strategic issues. Most groups have a tendency to get bogged down in operational concerns—probably because those are the easy problems to tackle.

Sixth, strategic change will likely require that you reorganize and put different people in key positions. But as critical as reorganization is, it should always follow and support the strategic plan, not precede or direct it. Finally, the CEO must have unwavering conviction about the strategy or it will not succeed. I am not presumptuous enough to assume that we have all the answers when it comes to strategic planning simply because we've been through a lengthy and comprehensive process. But I do believe that our experiences parallel those of many other U.S.-based manufacturing companies and can therefore be of some use to other companies striving to improve their competitive position in the global marketplace.

Dale Lang, Chairman, Lang Communications Inc.

> It was astounding to me that a company [3M] that large and that successful had never had any formal approach to strategy before.

Dale Lang, an entrepreneur in the true sense of the word, has built two innovative media companies. The first, Media Networks, was based on a concept that allowed companies to buy advertising space in national publications such as *Time, Newsweek, U.S. News and World Report,* and *Sports Illustrated* on a metro basis. The company grew rapidly, and was eventually acquired by 3M, where Mr. Lang became the company's largest employee shareholder. He was appointed to the newly formed Strategic Planning Committee when the company first began a systematic approach to planning. It was then that he encountered DPI's Strategic Thinking Process, which was used throughout 3M to create coherent corporate and division strategies.

However, despite the culture of innovation at 3M, Lang once again felt the tug of independence and went to work full-time on *Working Woman,* a magazine he had acquired some time before. This successful publication formed the basis of his second media venture, Lang Communications, which also owns *Ms., Sassy, Success,* and *Working Mother.*

Realizing the immediate need to develop a clear strategic mission for *Working Woman,* Lang brought in DPI to facilitate the process. We asked Mr. Lang to provide some insight into his experiences with strategic issues in this recent interview.

DPI: When did you first discover the Strategic Thinking Process?

DL: I really became exposed to all this while I was division vice president at 3M and was also on the corporate Strategic Planning Committee at 3M. There were a half dozen of us on that committee, and it was the first time that 3M had ever established such a group. The chairman picked the members to go on the committee, and we were charged with looking at strategic planning for the corporation as a whole.

I was there at the birth of strategic planning at 3M. And it was kind of astounding to me at the time that a company that large and that successful had really never had any kind of formal approach to strategy before. So I immersed myself deeply in it, and I became a true believer in what it could accomplish—the importance of it—as we all did in the company. It worked so well for us that we put all of our divisions through the Strategic Thinking drill.

Then when I left 3M, I went to work full-time on a magazine I had purchased.

DPI: This was *Working Woman?*

DL: Yes, *Working Woman* was a property I had purchased while I was at 3M. I'd staffed it with some good people that I knew but had only spent a little supervisory time on it on weekends.

I had a publisher and a full staff running it. But then when I joined the magazine and got inside with it, I saw that they were, as Mike [Robert] says, being seduced by opportunities left and right. They were trying to promote *Working Woman* centers, *Working Woman* seminars, *Working Woman* tapes, *Working Woman* videos...they were trying to do a whole list of outside programs that were related to the basic magazine, but not related to publishing. They were not concentrating and focusing on the magazine itself to make it as strong and healthy as possible.

I knew I couldn't just tell everybody "OK we're not going to do that kind of stuff anymore, we're all going to focus on the magazine. We're in a highly competitive world of magazines, and unless our magazine is really strong and focused, somebody's going to eat our lunch here. We can't be off chasing these other things and diluting our efforts that have to go in the magazine."

If I just arbitrarily said that to them, I'd get a lot of flak about it. One of the things about dealing with a magazine is that you're dealing with professional people...well-educated, talented people who are essentially your peers in the business and you happen to be the boss. They, however, regard themselves as being as knowledgeable about the business as you are. So it's hard to be arbitrary with them about something like that. I knew that one of the wonderful by-products of the DPI process was that everybody comes to the same conclusions at the end of it and owns that conclusion as their own. So one of the prime reasons I wanted to put the magazine through it was to get to that common decision. And I was confident that, having gone through it so many times at 3M, I knew what kind of a course it would take. I was certain that if we examined all the factors that affect our business in a systematic manner, we could chart our course and these different people would all come to the same place. I felt rather confident that they would come to the same conclusion I was already coming to.

DPI: And they did?

DL: Yes. And it set the stage so that I didn't have to be arbitrary. I didn't have to say, "Just do it. You've got to just cut the budget. You can't spend any more than this. Just do what I say."

DPI: How did the group deal with the concept of driving force?

DL: It was complicated. A magazine, of course, is selling to the reader, the subscriber, the newsstand buyer, and to the advertiser. And you can have a little different strategy with each and obviously a different approach to each. And they had some trouble with homing in on the driving force because of that. You see, that was the crux of what I was saying earlier. If you say we're the *Working Woman* information center, we would disseminate media to working women. We'd do it in the form of tapes, videos, magazines, movies, newsletters, and other such things.

DPI: That would make the company user class–driven, providing a variety of products and services to a specific target group.

DL: That's right. But if you say we are a magazine company focusing on publishing magazines for a specific set of readers, your driving force changes to one driven by product, which changes the scope of products, users, and markets you will operate with and in.

DPI: One of your first questions to DPI was whether the strategy process would work in a small company. What's the difference between the way it works in a small company versus a larger one such as 3M?

DL: It's different because you're involving more grass-root people at a smaller company, and you know that to get a good group together you're involving more people who are not management people. At a company like 3M, the people involved are all managers. At the magazine, we had some other types of people...circulation people, the advertising manager, even the lead salesperson.

DPI: People who aren't accustomed to thinking strategically.

DL: Also editors and art directors. That was really the shocking part, because these people generally regard themselves as simply talent, who think they are just paid to create and they are not usually involved in making decisions on the business side.

My competitors generally do not involve their editors in anything like this; they just keep them isolated. But I found by bringing them into this process, it worked very well because it let them really see the other side of the magazine. It also gave them an appreciation for the problems that the other sides, the advertising side or the production side or circulation side, had.

I followed up on the Strategic Thinking Process with a management meeting structure. I meet monthly to review the magazine: the performance of the magazine against plan and against last year. That's not so unusual, but it is unusual to bring editors into that meeting and hold them responsible for their budget and have them listen to the ad director report on how she performed against her budget and so forth. And it generally made for a much closer family and much more cooperation, so it was a very healthy result.

Mark Ungerer, Vice Chairman, FLEXcon Inc.

I learned more about our company today than I have during the past several years put together.

Mark Ungerer was president of FLEXcon, a supplier of pressure-sensitive film lamination to the graphic arts industry, and is now its vice chairman. Privately held, the company employs about 1000 people at several locations and is headquartered in Spencer, Massachusetts.

DPI: How would you describe the state of your business prior to beginning DPI's Strategic Thinking Process?

MU: Strictly seat-of-the-pants. We simply did things the way we had always done them. There was no formal planning, and managers worked independently with little knowledge of, or interest in, what the others were doing. It's almost embarrassing to think about how apart we were—though we *thought* we were together.

DPI: What key needs were you trying to address?

MU: We wanted to get everyone to pull in the same direction. We needed to include all key people in the decision-making process. We had been "tellers": "do this" or "do that."

DPI: What element of DPI's process did you find most important?

MU: Believe it or not, it was putting our thoughts on sheets and tacking them to the walls! The process forced us to do what we should have been doing all along. Looking at all those issues staring us in the face forced out a collective "wow!" We were finally able to address our key management concerns and measure our progress in a systematic way.

DPI: What were your impressions of the first three-day session and its output?

MU: We were absolutely amazed. So much was done is such a short time. Moreover, the group's feeling of involvement and learning about ourselves was great. Some really good people emerged whom we didn't even know about. One key manager said, "I learned more about our company today than I have during the past several years put together." We all felt like that.

DPI: What are some of the most significant results that the process of Strategic Thinking has brought to your organization?

MU: There are three that readily come to mind. First, is the best harmony we've ever had among our top 30 people. Second, we have been able to crystallize real issues that we can get our teeth into and act on. Third, we need DPI and its excellent outside facilitation to play an ongoing role. It's easy to think that you can do this yourself. You can't.

DPI: Can you provide some specific examples of change that resulted from the process?

MU: Here are two quick ones that reaped tremendous benefits. We established a "linkage manager" to be a liaison between our U.S. headquarters and European operations. He was identified, recruited, and hired within weeks of our decision to implement, and he spent substantial time in both operations as part of his training. Now, the cooperation and coordination between the two units is better than ever, resulting in substantial increases in productivity and efficiency. In another dramatic instance, we improved our forecasting accuracy to the extent that we can now invest excess cash for the maximum possible return—before, we often had to call-in investments to cover shortages in cashflow. Those days are long gone, and we get the best possible return from all of our investment opportunities.

DPI: How much progress, in your words, has been made between the first Strategic Thinking session and today, as compared with an equivalent period of time prior to that first session?

MU: There's just one word for it: tremendous. We've made simply tremendous strides.

DPI: There are a multitude of approaches today to Strategic Thinking. What was it about DPI's approach that made it distinct from the others?

MU: The difference is that DPI takes a "complicated" topic and makes it easy to deal with. And I'm convinced that this can't be done well without an outside facilitator, and DPI provides the absolute best. We need a periodic "temperature taking," and DPI knows how to do this quickly, accurately, and constructively.

DPI: What other comments would you like to make to your colleagues reading this interview?

MU: Normally, people like Mike Robert and firms like DPI are a "flash in the pan." They're gone before you know it, and a lot of money has been spent for very little progress. With Mike and DPI, the longer you're with them, the better it is, which is quite rare. The more you use them, the more depth you're able to achieve in terms of using the processes to penetrate the organization. Mike and DPI are significant contributors to us at FLEXcon, and would be significant contributors to *anyone* who avails himself and his company of their services.

Gary Holland, President and CEO, DataCard Corporation

I was astonished that our senior management group had no concept of our strategy.

Gary Holland, 49, has been CEO since March 1988, when he was elevated from president and COO by a German firm that served as DataCard's "white knight," saving it from a hostile takeover attempt. The company had been through "two or three cycles of senior management" in Gary's words, and had traditionally been heavily sales driven, with an emphasis on growth for growth's sake.

"It was a challenge," relates Holland, "to determine just how we had gotten into so much trouble and where we ought to be going. As you can imagine, the takeover attempt and resultant new owners had a dramatic impact on senior management, with many people leaving and those who remained comprising a highly sober group."

Holland had been a strategic planner for another firm in the late 1970s (he joined DataCard in 1982). He became familiar with a wide range of strategy options and then, as president of another high-tech firm in 1979, found himself in the position of being the one responsible for planning, implementing, and achieving growth goals. During that period he became acquainted with the concept of a "driving force" determining the nature and direction of a business.

"As a new CEO of DataCard," he says, "I knew I had to draw upon my past strategy experience to assemble and give direction to my senior management. I also had to apprise the new board of directors of our intended direction, and I simply didn't have much time to do it. It was at that juncture that I came across Mike Robert's book *The Strategist CEO,* in which I learned about DPI's approaches to strategy and how similar they were to my own."

The staff urged Holland to conduct the strategy sessions himself, but he thought that the team would be better served with a facilitator. Today, everyone would agree with him. "You see, the DPI process itself wasn't a radical change for us," he explains. "But with DPI facilitators running the sessions, we were able to get so much more out of the approach than if we had tried to do it ourselves. Our owners, particularly, are *very* pleased."

It appears that the most helpful aspect at the outset was creating a unified vision. The company had been pursuing a market category–driven philosophy, and the company had made several divestitures and acquisitions in line with that strategy. "We had acquired some key players in our market," says Holland. "In the first two to three hours of the meeting with DPI, I was astonished that our senior management group had *no concept* of our strategy and disagreed with it once they learned of it! I was happy about DPI's intervention because, at the conclusion, we all knew about and agreed with our strategy—there was absolutely no question about our beliefs and direction. For example, we set clear priorities on our customers, employees, vendors, owners, and local communities, in that order."

The advice that Holland has for others in similar situations is surprisingly simple. "Don't expect too much," he warns. "It's been very positive for us because we had realistic expectations, limited our objectives, and communicated them to DPI. It's imperative to be realistic. There is enough concrete output to please the most driving pragmatist, but also sufficient conceptual buy-in to please the visionaries."

One of the great ironies about the DataCard experience is that the company had on its board two members (of two "big 10" consulting firms specializing in strategy). "They really had to be convinced!" reports Holland. But once they understood that DPI was not there to write a strategy, but rather to provide a process whereby DataCard senior management would create its own strategy, objections disappeared. In fact, both of these board members are now strong supporters. "They wish DPI were here continually," observes Holland with some glee.

Not everyone was so easily won over. Holland feels that he would have been more precise about the "preconditioning" of his management team if he were to start all over again. "I should have told them more about what it was I wanted to accomplish. Many were initially concerned about the 'waste of time' until we were well into the process. My senior man from the United Kingdom flew home, he later admitted, telling everyone in sight that 'these Americans are absolutely crazy!' He was one of the last to come around!

"DPI's approach is simply different from anything else we've been through. I'm a big supporter, and we're actively examining other services DPI can provide us. For example, we can certainly use a periodic 'strategic' checkup."

DataCard and Gary Holland have found that careful attention to strategy, and avoiding being absorbed in the tactical problems of the daily business, had paid off handsomely. He attributes this in no small manner to DataCard's transition, through the process, from a group of seven or eight product-driven units to an organization driven by its market category. "It was dramatic to watch the group begin planning for an approach in the market that placed a premium on selling solutions, concepts, and problem solving for customers," he reports. Through better business management and some intelligent acquisitions, DataCard has grown from $225 million to about $500 million over the last three years. There's no arguing with that direction.

United Grain Growers

The Problem

It was at a critical point in the company's history when Brian Hayward was elected CEO by the board of United Grain Growers (UGG) in January 1991 and Ted Allen became chairman.

The billion-dollar Canadian grain cooperative was wrestling with shifts in the business environment that would force it to effect some fundamental changes in the way the company had done business for 85 years—just to maintain margins Hayward described as "razor thin." And one of the primary challenges would be to bridge a communications gap that had developed over time between the board and management.

"Our board of directors was very unhappy with the profitability of our company and the way it was being managed," says Ted Allen, UGG's chairman. Things had to change. At the same time there was a growing frustration and uneasiness among managers who believed they were getting mixed signals from the board as to its direction and wishes.

As a farm cooperative, UGG's core business is to provide a variety of production, handling and marketing services to its customers and shareholders—grain farmers in western Canadian provinces. Created by the government in 1906, it is an agent of the quasi-government Canadian Wheat Board. As such, it is subject to extensive regulation and depends to some measure on government support, yet competes for its business with several other co-ops.

Eighty-five percent of UGG's business is in grain handling and marketing. The company also provides a variety of other services that help farmers to improve production and add value to the finished product.

The evolution of UGG's business took many years to develop and found its way into a lot of loosely related businesses, as Ted Allen explains. "In the late, late years of the 1800s and the first few years of the 1900s in western Canada, there was a collusion between the railway companies—aided and abetted by the railways—through something called the *Car Order Book,* where a farmer couldn't get a transport for his grain unless he participated in the system that had been created. There was a case that went all the way to the Supreme Court of Canada that overrode the situation, and in 1906, United Grain Growers was formed as a company of farmers to market this grain. UGG also provided over the years a grain handling service. A tremendous diversity of services to farmers developed gradually. These services always seemed to be related to farming, but they sold such things as lumber, coal, apples, sewing machines, and farm machinery. As the need for a particular service arose, we got into this tremendous thing."

Among these "add-ons" are seed research, farm magazine publishing, oilseed crushing, fertilizer, and feed distribution, among others. Some of these ventures have been successful, and others have lost money for many years. In better times, the "losers" could be viewed as "strategic initiatives" or simply as necessary "overhead." But as times have changed and competitive, market, and regulatory environments have changed with them, some of these ventures have become expensive and unnecessary drains on the company's resources. So the central questions Hayward and Allen faced in early 1991 were: "Which of our many ventures are necessary to support our core business? And what, after all, is at the core of our business—our driving force? The physical assets? The farmer constituents? And what's the balance of priorities strategically when our management makes its day-to-day operational decisions?" The need to find answers to these questions began to come to a head almost immediately after Allen and Hayward took their new positions.

"One of the first things that landed on my desk was a report recommending that we put a couple of million dollars into a new web press at our printing plant," Brian Hayward recalls. "But we had already lost a lot of money on that operation, and I didn't think we really knew what we were doing."

That report went right to the heart of the challenge at hand. It posed basic strategic questions with important operational implications, as Hayward points out: "People in management were getting increasingly frustrated. They would ask themselves: `Why are we doing some of these things? Why are we looking at putting more money into printing when I'm having a tough time here running the country grain elevator business?' Real frustration."

Part of the problem, Hayward realized, was that management perceived "little direction from the top. So you, as a manager, could do whatever you wanted. You had a lot of autonomy, but after a while it was like letting your kids eat all the candy they wanted. After a while you'd say: `What am I really trying to achieve with respect to the whole? Where do I fit into the whole scheme of the company?' There wasn't one vision. We had fragmented individual communications between board members and managers."

Managers found themselves reacting based on individual interpretations of their personal communications with board members.

"Board members exercise absolutely no authority on their own behalf, and management people sometimes forget that." Allen states, "The board members' power resides only in their ability to influence decisions of the board, sitting as a body, or through powers delegated to them by the board.

"In order for a board of directors and senior management to work together in a productive and harmonious manner, I think it is absolutely critical that all participants have a crystal-clear understanding of their roles. Nature abhors a vacuum, and senior managers and boards are powerful and aggressive people. If there is weakness or indecision in one group, the other group will move in and usurp their power."

The board at UGG is composed of 12 shareholder farmers. "These are not a bunch of hayseeds," Allen points out. "Two-thirds of them are university graduates; a number of them run their own businesses with sales in seven figures. And a number of them are on the boards of large companies."

Somewhere along the line, communication between the board and management had broken down. Managers were unclear as to the board's wishes, and the board was increasingly uneasy with the way the company was being managed.

The Turnaround

Allen and Hayward quickly recognized the need to open up communication and establish a clear consensus on strategy if they were to get the board and management headed down the same road together.

"We needed a process," says Hayward, "where we could all find a common direction. I didn't want to come in as a dictator and say, 'OK, here's what we're going to do.' I had seen so much fragmentation and lack of unity that even before I was officially in place, I contacted DPI."

Among a variety of other actions and initiatives aimed at establishing a unified vision, UGG enlisted the aid of Decision Processes International, having become aware of the effectiveness of its Strategic Thinking Process in bringing groups together to debate strategic issues in an organized manner and arrive at a consensus.

"What it boiled down to ultimately," reports Hayward, "was a debate as to whether the physical assets are really what we're in business for. Or is the farmer our reason to be?" This is a basic question facing all grain co-ops in Canada today, and UGG has established its own direction in that regard.

"Our competitors' position on these issues reflects a mindset that says, `The fundamental job of the board of directors is the preservation of the asset base—especially the physical assets.' Today we've got quite a bit of consolidation going on in the industry, and more that needs to be done. For example, not long ago we had six thousand country elevators in western Canada. Most people believe that two hundred would service the industry adequately.

"We are what you may perceive as a right wing co-op," says Allen, somewhat tongue-in-cheek. "We believe in the marketplace. We believe that less government is better government, and we believe in enterprise, initiative, and innovation. And unlike other co-ops, we do not lock-in our customers. They're free to get a better deal someplace else if they wish. So it's up to us to provide them with a greater value than they can get elsewhere.

"Anyway I think our perspective as the UGG board is that our paramount responsibilities are to see that the business adapts to the times and prospers and meets the demands of the customers, and in that way ensure its survival. I think we see that preservation of physical assets is less of a priority."

In the course of the three days of the Strategic Thinking Process, issues such as these were subject to open debate between the 12-person board and top management.

The group succeeded at establishing a clear consensus on a strategy and a business concept that all could agree on. "Finally we said `We're driven by our customer base—the farmers—that's our reason to be, not our production capacity or the physical assets needed to support it,'" Hayward concludes.

Under the banner "Meeting Farmers' Business Needs," the company has established for itself a unified vision of its future shape and purpose. As an integral part of the Strategic Thinking Process, the team defines a set of critical issues that must be resolved to make it happen.

"I was surprised at the commonality on the concept of driving force," Hayward now reflects, "but no one had ever pulled the entire board-management group together and gone through the issues the way we did."

Since January 1991, UGG has divested two problematic and money-draining operations—the printing plant and an oilseed crushing operation. They've established management targets and lines of communications that didn't exist before. A database has been developed to better target customers and their needs; a quality program and a training and development strategy are in place.

Armed with a clear business concept, management now knows how to allocate resources in order to support the driving force of the business. Management and the members of the board have a firm understanding as to the future shape of UGG and its goals in terms of serving its customers. But most important, they have come to the realization that "Meeting Farmers' Business Needs" depends on customer loyalty, customer service, and understanding what the farmers' business needs really are.

"Our people are going to be critical to making that happen," says Hayward. "They need the tools, the support, and the communication from us. And we've got to keep the board and management team communicating with each other."

Kurt Wiedenhaupt, President and CEO, AEG Corporation

I recognized that a unified strategy for the eight groups would be absolutely critical to success.

In December 1989, AEG purchased three automation businesses from Westinghouse Electric. These companies—Westinghouse Drive Control Systems, Westinghouse Factory Automation

Systems, and Mictron—nicely complemented AEG's family of five other automation companies, creating a "critical mass" of capabilities unmatched in the U.S. industrial automation marketplace. A new entity called AEG Westinghouse Industrial Automation Corporation was formed.

The challenge since then has been to forge a single strategy—a partnership—among these eight units. AEG's chosen path is, in CEO Kurt Wiedenhaupt's words, "to offer comprehensive, state-of-the-art solutions to the automation market."

As many who have gone down similar roads know, this is far easier said than done.

At the outset, Wiedenhaupt recognized that a unified strategy for the eight groups would be absolutely critical to success. One of his first actions following the Westinghouse acquisitions, then, was to bring in a DPI partner to take 25 key people from the various units through the DPI Strategic Thinking Process. We asked Wiedenhaupt to give us some insight into the process and his experiences to date.

DPI: Maybe we should start with a picture of your business concept and the market situation it addresses.

KW: It is a very tough market, and we are trying an approach that is not American, like apple pie and ice cream. AEG by tradition is a systems, a solution company in the field of industrial automation. And the American way of approaching the market has most of the time been to buy hardware, get together with a software supplier, have a systems integrator, then patch the thing together. The responsibility for success or failure lies more or less with the customer instead of the supplier. Or a smaller business might use a systems integrator who may not have the financial resources to provide complete support.

Here you have a financially strong company like AEG saying we take responsibility for the solution. We supply the hardware. We supply the software. We supply the integration, the service, the start-up. Tell us what you want to achieve. We will go back and design the whole system. There will be a very close cooperation with your engineers because in the end it must be your installation and not something we think you need. But then, thereafter, it's our responsibility.

DPI: Is this unique among your competitors?

KW: It is definitely not common. In certain specific areas and niches you have people who have done it and done it successfully. Some companies are trying to address the problem by forming alliances. But when you look at some of these companies and see how many alliances they have, you find a list worthy of the Yellow Pages. They are working today with this company because it suits them, tomorrow with that company because it suits them. They can never develop a consistent approach to a systems solution or develop standard applications packages.

DPI: What actions have you taken so far to make this synergy happen, and why was it so important to bring the key players together with DPI's assistance to develop their own common strategy?

KW: We are reducing our eight units to a smaller number. Whenever you consolidate operations you have to involve people in the decision-making process. Integration is hard anyhow, but it would be even more difficult without the cooperation of the people who will be affected.

DPI: Has this approach been successful so far?

KW: The DPI process is still going on, but it was a full success. We pulled the people together. We helped them understand their differences. To understand each other's business. Without forcing it, people developed a desire to identify not their differences but their commonalities. They pulled together a vision and developed a mission statement for all of them. That is the expression of unity. They worked together on the critical issues. And we realize that even though we are working in several marketplaces, there are overriding issues that are critical for all of them. And they all agreed on these critical issues. So it is a process of integration. It is a process of clear definition, of bringing clarity into the minds of the participants. It is a process that is simple. The company now has a strategic plan which they took part in formulating. So it is not something that has been introduced to them by the owner or by somebody because he can speak better or he happens to have a certain position. No. Twenty-five people worked on that process together. Twenty-five key people from all parts of the operations. It is now their strategy.

DPI: How soon after these acquisitions did you begin, and what kinds of results have you seen to date?

KW: We started a month after the acquisition, which was December 1989. It is now less than a year. Half a year. And I can only say that people are amazed at how much we have achieved in such a short period of time. The eight units will be four very shortly. Our savings, generated out of that process, in overhead, are between $2 and $3 million a year. The market, our customers, has reacted very positively to what we are doing. And this is expressed in the orders and the responses we get. Since we have gone through the process, since we have acquired these companies and have given them a clear mission, one company's inquiry rate from December to now has tripled! The business volume in all units has dramatically increased, which is not a surprise to us but a very pleasant confirmation that our efforts went in the right direction.

DPI: Do you have any comment on the DPI Strategic Thinking Process itself?

KW: Number one, it is no mumbo jumbo. It is straight, may I say, street wisdom. It is not an academic challenge to the participants. It is clearly, simply an application of sound, basic business knowledge. The difference is that DPI's people are not telling us what our business should be or is like. We make these assessments. It is our process. DPI says to us, "We are giving you a road map, but you have to do the walking. You have to identify where you are. You have to identify where you want to be. And we are helping you to make sure that you're not running in circles, and that you get from A to B. And even there, we are helping you to identify yourself the best way to get from A to B."

DPI: How is this different from other approaches you've observed?

KW: I've seen too many products from strategy specialists that are extremely impressive, especially when they are bound in brown leather with a company logo on top. But they don't translate these strategies into action. The DPI process provides practical, down-to-earth actions that move you toward your strategic goal. It's simple. To the point. Convincing. Action oriented. I'm not saying that these other processes are intellectually bad. They might even be more sophisticated than the DPI process. I only can say that for me it's not decisive how sophisticated a process is but how effective it is.

Odey Powers, Chairman, Nicolet Instrument Corporation

The result for us was that some of the best thoughts came from people who were not ranking executives.

DPI: What was the state of your business before you started the Strategic Thinking Process?

OP: I had just come to Nicolet, and it was in difficult condition. The industry it serves is a very highly competitive industry, and some of the previous folks who were managing it had lost their way, so we were in need of turning it around. We were probably a year and a half into that process, and whenever you're in a turnaround mode, your focus is almost always tactical, never strategic. It had become apparent to us that we were in that circumstance. We were resolving most of the short-term issues, beginning to get the business turned around, and were going to be profitable.

We soon recognized that our need was not simply to get people thinking about strategic issues. We also needed to enable our people to act strategically, and to focus the management. DPI's Strategic Thinking Process accomplished all of these objectives *and* was a great team-building experience.

DPI: What experience did your people have with strategy development?

OP: When we began to rebuild this company, we had 12 vice presidents, and within 12 months all those were gone and we had 12 new ones. Consequently we had a variety of different experiences, some of which were not applicable. Some of these people had established their own belief system concerning strategic planning. DPI offered us new definitions that gave us a common language with a different view, which was very proactive. The process is very simple, but it is very, very effective. It identifies those things that have to be evaluated before you can think strategically. The whole process gets you into a mode where you can now think strategically. It doesn't hand you a strategic plan. It just gives your management team the means, the process you need to creative strategic plans yourselves. I've gone through two or three different approaches to strategic planning with some other consulting groups, but I've found that none of the others were as effective in setting the groundwork for people to ultimately become real strategists.

DPI: Why did you need a facilitator in conducting the Strategic Thinking Process? Couldn't you have done it yourselves?

OP: I think it's easy to get off track. In any organization there are always people who speak more forcefully than others. It also precludes the CEO and the top executives from lording over what they believe is their dominion. DPI's process kind of strips you down where you don't really have a lot of rank. Your thought process is the thing that defends you. The result for us was that some of our best thoughts came from people who weren't high-ranking officers.

DPI: It drew those people out?

OP: Absolutely. We got some new ideas, some new thinking from areas I never expected to hear from—new thinking that had never even been addressed. And it came from all the folks in the process. We had 50 people on our strategic committee. That in and of itself was something to orchestrate. But since I was trying to team-build, I asked DPI to indulge me and let me make the group as big as I could so that we could get as many people thinking strategically as possible.

DPI: This may seem like a simplistic question, but why do you think it's important for people to think strategically within an organization?

OP: Well, you're right, it sounds academic, but it isn't. The question is a good one. In other words, to the extent that you're running a good shop and you're making money, why start doing all this?

The answer is that a clear strategy has far more impact on short-term thinking than you think. If you have a good strategic plan, you're not making wasteful use of resources on a short-term basis. And, certainly, one of the basic challenges involved in refocusing the company is to know what we are, and maybe even more valuable, what we are not. We were spending an awful lot of money on things that we were not. It was just wasted money, in engineering time, in capital asset resources, in MIS programs—frankly pursuing something that never could be.

And so without strategic thinking you can be very, very wasteful, and provide your competitor with an awful lot of advantages while you're floundering around trying to find what it is you want to be. And he already knows.

DPI: Your competitors already know what you are and are not?

OP: You bet. And that's another thing that's unique about the DPI Strategic Thinking Process. It makes you think in terms of what you think your competitor's strategy is. That's a new experience I'd never had. It was a compelling exercise.

DPI: What kind of company is Nicolet?

OP: Nicolet is in the electronic instruments business. We serve primarily three markets—the analytical chemical field, the biomedical field, and finally the more dicey competitive business called test and measurement. This is simply a business where we gather signals.

You've seen oscilloscopes. Well, this is the high side of that, the scientific side of the oscilloscope business where we gather wave forms and identify phenomena from electrical signals. The common denominator of all this is that we take any form of an analog signal—whether it be light, temperature, pressure, sound, anything that forms an analog signal—and translate that analog signal into a digit. We can translate every one of these signals into some kind of a digit that can be processed by a computer, and you can do a multiplicity of things once you get it into that form. So it's a technical business and we, without question, came to the conclusion through the DPI process that we are technology driven. A year later we modified it to say we're *applied technology driven.* That modification became extremely important because a technology-driven company seemingly would suggest one who's in basic research. We are not in the basic research business at all. Basic research is being done by the scientific labs. Our business is applying that technology to the needs of our markets. But we have about 45 or 50 Ph.D. mathematicians, physicists, and chemists here. We have about 110 or so people with masters degrees, and they are fundamentally directed toward resolving problems through electronics that customers would have in our marketplaces. The end product is some form of low-volume, premium-priced product that solves a customer problem.

DPI: What kind of competitive situation are you in? Is it a very competitive type of industry?

OP: Well, the truth is, that's one of the reasons strategic thinking is necessary for us. There are very large competitors in all of the fields we're in. We have adopted the "niche market" approach simply because if you get into any of these markets with higher volume products, then you play into somebody's else's strategy, which is to drive production costs down and sell at low prices. That's not our bag. We're anything but a low-cost production house. And so our whole strategy is to be a source of *solutions* to customers and produce premium products, with applications support in the aftermarket. Our customers are those that are willing to pay a premium for our services. So we have many competitors that are in marketplaces we serve, but we try to stay in niches where they are not. We try to be pretty loose in our shoes to strategically stay where we know our strengths really are. To maintain this stance, it is very important, as I said before, that we know what we are not. You can be trapped into believing that because a competitor appears to be in the same business we are, we have to attack them where they are.

We've gotten ourselves into businesses where a competitor had great manufacturing strength and all we really did was depreciate all of the money we made in the areas where we do have good niche success. You lose all in those areas where you have no place to play.

DPI: Can you, at this stage, point to any tangible results?

OP: Well, we're better focused, there's a willingness to take risks now for longer term benefits than we were willing to do before. Before we were concentrating on putting out fires. Now there's a commitment to the future beyond the coming quarter by people who had never thought strategically. And without any question there is a more efficient use of available funds.

One reason is that without any long-term strategic view, people, when they see that their short-term bonuses may be impacted by an expenditure that they can't see any immediate result from, are less likely to concentrate on that task. The outgrowth of this new strategic thinking among our people is that, for example, 50 percent of all our sales last year came from products that are only 18 months old. And that's because our people are now more willing to risk money on new products. It's now very clear that the only way we can grow the business and make provision for future bonuses is to put money in on a short-term basis that have long-term benefits. They know that management will support them all the way because we are all in this thing together.

And we just came off another straight quarter of record profits!

Larry Smith, Managing Director, Castrol (U.K.) Limited

People were under the illusion that as a company we were actually doing quite well.

The Castrol name is a familiar one to anyone who has watched an auto race. As the world's leading lubricants specialist, Castrol has carved out a unique niche among oil companies over the past 90 years.

But leadership is not always forever, and when Larry Smith became managing director of Castrol's U.K. unit in 1990, he found an eroding market position and a lack of a strategic direction.

In an interview with DPI, Mr. Smith discussed the steps he took to refocus Castrol U.K.'s strategy and the role that DPI's Strategic Thinking Process played in returning Castrol to the winner's circle.

DPI: When you became managing director, what state did you find the company in?

LS: Castrol U.K. had been successful over the years. We've been around over 90 years, and through the 1970s and into the early 1980s, had actually done a very good job. When I arrived here and started looking around, I found that declining profits and market share were major problems. One of the things that I detected, apart from the lack of direction (or maybe because of the lack of direction), was a complacent, almost arrogant, attitude that we are good, we're well known, we're well respected, brand leader, market leader, etc.

I think there was a loss of commitment to the longer-term development of the business. The effect of this has been that in recent years we've been leap-frogged in some of the product areas where traditionally we've led the market. This flies in the face of our need to maintain our historic position as the leading lubricants specialist. I think that one of the biggest problems was that there wasn't the longer-term vision of what we're trying to do, what makes the business tick, and what's going to keep us driving forward. It is fair to say that the business gradually declined without it being noticed.

DPI: Why do you think this decline took place?

LS: There wasn't an overriding strategy for the company that could permeate its way down the organization, to develop a common understanding of what the company was trying to do. I think that was what was missing. We were trying to do the things we'd been doing in the past which had relied on market volume growth; however, this volume growth had disappeared in the last decade. In fact, in a lot of the areas, the markets were declining. They don't use as much oil, and there are some quite considerable market shifts in types of products and even between markets.

DPI: What did you do to begin rectifying the situation?

LS: I tracked the last 10 years and put them up on graphs, and even the management people were horrified. People were under the illusion that as a company we were actually doing quite well. And it was only when it was put in front of them for the first time that they realized we hadn't been doing very well at all. In fact, we had been doing quite badly. At the same time, I might add, we were getting into a recession in the United Kingdom, so the future didn't look particularly rosy, either.

We are in a situation where we are the leader by a long way; we've got high market shares and declining margins operating in a static market. To get any sort of future growth out of the business, we need a somewhat radical approach.

DPI: Once you identified the need to refocus your strategy, what attracted you to the DPI Strategic Thinking Process?

LS: First, the sheer fact that there is a process. The fact that it is a fairly simple process was very attractive; there's nothing fancy about it, it's very logical and very simply presented. Start from a simple base, just keep adding to it, double-check, recheck, does it still fit, carry on. There really were two things there that were critical to us. One was the process, the actual documentation and the discipline of managing the meetings, and the other one was the facilitator role. I needed somebody to act as controller or arbiter, and that really had to be an external person. I did actually have a couple of options. One was to do it myself, which concerned me for a number of reasons. I didn't want to dictate to the other management people what the new strategy should be or dominate the process so that it appeared to be my strategy and not theirs. As individuals I wanted them to participate, be committed collectively as a management team, and feel that this is our business. I could actually have pulled in a couple of people from inside the organization to facilitate, but I just felt that I needed somebody who understood the process, and I needed third-party credibility.

Also, I like the fact that everything that was documented and discussed came out of our mouths, and it was what we said. If it had been presented or controlled like a traditional consultant, it would not have had any credibility whatsoever. The thing I enjoyed about the DPI approach was that we have ownership of our strategy. And I think DPI's facilitating was crucial to the success of it.

DPI: Were there any surprises as you evaluated your business?

LS: One of the interesting observations after a couple of days, and the thing that surprised us, was the realization that we didn't have to change the business we're in. We had the expectation that the basis of our business did have to change—one, because the company was in trouble and, two, because we had gone through this glorious process. At the end of the day we found that we're actually in the right business after all. What we were trying to do as a company was correct; it was the way we were doing it that was wrong. We actually have operational problems.

DPI: So do you find that by refocusing your strategy that you've gained the ability to prioritize and begin to solve those operational problems?

LS: Yes. In fact, it gives us focus on the operational problems. The ability to prioritize them is how it starts to manifest itself. Obviously, in terms of the strategy, it is now better documented, better thought through, it's more detailed, and people have got ownership and commitment to it.

One element of this process that certainly did help was the development of a list of critical issues. We have worked our way through those. We originally came up with something like 15 highly critical issues of which 7 have already been resolved or incorporated into the normal operating part of the business. However, as we progress new ones emerge and we add them to the list. So at least we're moving on and focusing on critical issues. I think maybe that is a barometer of success. We have, in fact, tackled some of the critical issues and can now identify other ones that are important to our strategy.

DPI: How was the concept of driving force received by the group?

LS: That was an interesting one. We have had the misapprehension that we are a marketing company. We've used that terminology for a long time, particularly over the last 20 years. We have believed we are a marketing company. I've always had a lot of concerns about that. Mistakenly we've tried to devise a marketing mystique that has tended to become a bit academic. Through the DPI process, it became clear that we're product-driven not user class–driven. It made us sit up and realize that it was the product development over the years that had in fact been our corporate strength. We had always done well when we had the right products. Over the years people had lost sight of this important fact; instead, we had been looking at the cost base, head count, and all sorts of things, and neglecting product development.

After a fair bit of discussion we did agree that in terms of DPI's definitions, we are certainly not user class–driven. We only develop and sell lubricants and related products. We do not identify a market and supply all of its needs. What we do is identify different market segments that require specialized lubricants and set out to sell only lubricants and related products and services.

DPI: Has this clear understanding of your corporate strategy had an impact on how you allocate resources?

LS: Yes, among other things we've realized that we, in fact, need to reinvest in people in some of the customer/industry interfaces. To give you an example, we are very strong in the motor business, particularly retail trade and manufacturing. We've always had sizable departments of highly qualified people who were OEM [original equipment manufacturer] coordinators. They were in constant contact and would know what the customers were looking at and how we could assist them, whether it be in the vehicle or in the manufacturing process. However, those areas have been run down over the years. We now realize that those areas have to be reinstated if we want to stay in a market (which is another element of the DPI process, "do you or don't you?"). We've got to develop it properly, and we need to put the necessary resources into it.

DPI: What results have you seen, if any, to date—either tangible or intangible?

LS: Well, in the short term and for the long term we do have a clear direction. I was at a meeting even this morning to put our marketing plans together. They do not incorporate a five-year horizon. The guys were questioning whether or not these ambitious five-year targets are achievable. There was a realization that there is nothing wrong with the objectives as ambitious as they may appear. We've got to change our mindset. We must actually come up with the plans that will achieve the goals. There are ways of doing it, and we must go and find those ways.

Jim Buell, President and Owner, Domain Inc.

An ability to market animal feed and analyze forages has helped build Domain Inc. into a major animal nutrition company. But it has taken a different skill—a thought process called Strategic Thinking from Decision Processes International (DPI)—to articulate and clarify an identity and market emphasis for this New Richmond, Wisconsin, dairy farmer supplier and consultant.

"Up until a year ago, we were going in 10 different directions," says company president James H. Buell, who bought Domain in 1980. "We were aware of it, but never addressed the problem. We never stopped to ask ourselves whether we should allocate resources and develop expertise in specific market areas."

When a member of the board of directors asked him where the company would be in five years, Buell said he expected sales to be $80 million primarily generated from dairy producers. "It was a typical response expected from a financial person," he says. "What he really wanted to know was what the company was going to look like and how it was going to serve its markets. I hadn't thought of that and didn't know how to address the issue."

Direction and Consensus

Buell engaged the services of DPI convinced that the simplicity of the process and the help of a third-party facilitator would ferret out a specific purpose formulated and shared by the 15 members of his management team.

"The facilitator was a great asset," he says. "It would be very difficult for a person inside the company to lead a similar discussion because of a personal prejudice or lack of skill.

"As for the process, it gave everyone an opportunity to voice their ideas on various activities and markets. This was invaluable. Between what they thought the company was and what they thought I wanted it to be, we had quite a diversity of opinion."

Through formalized discussion, that diversity of opinion was transformed into a general consensus. A strategic profile and list of critical issues were drawn in support of a driving force geared to satisfying customer needs, and the result was a tremendous transition for the company.

An Animal Nutrition Company

"The profile has definitely clarified our markets," Buell says. "We were saying that we were a feed company or a dairy company serving our dealers. Our profile states that we are truly an animal nutrition company serving dairy producers. This notion has steered us away from nondairy markets, which has been a hell of a break for us."

Domain markets animal feed and preservatives nationwide under the trade names Duboy and Cure Crop. The company also offers on-farm technical support, such as nutritional analysis to help farmers obtain the highest possible payback on feed costs while meeting requirements for milk and egg production.

"The strategic profile has helped us tie our preservatives business with our animal nutrition business, clarify our market position in New York and California, strengthen our service activities, and increase direct work with the customer," Buell points out. "We use this profile on a day-to-day basis to assign manhours and allocate other resources in the proper areas."

The critical issues are evaluated during the company's regularly scheduled meetings, and Buell expects to update and replace them according to changes in the business.

So if you need to know how much you should feed a cow to get 50 pounds of milk per cow, per day, even five years from now, ask Jim Buell; he can tell you.

David Biorn, President and CEO, St. Luke's Health System Inc.

David Biorn took the helm of St. Luke's Regional Medical Center, a 353-bed hospital in Sioux City, Iowa, in a time of great upheaval in the health care industry. The forces of change affecting government regulation, insurance, technology, and delivery of services have created a new and challenging environment. As many hospitals struggle to survive, St. Luke's has prospered. A clearly focused strategy aided by DPI's Strategic Thinking Process is one of the key elements in the hospital's current success.

DPI: When did you first identify the need for a Strategic Thinking Process?

DB: As I was becoming acquainted with the organization, fairly quickly it occurred to me that we needed to focus our energies. I saw a lot of activity, but I didn't really know for sure whether it was all productive activity that would contribute to our business success.

DPI: What specifically attracted you to the DPI approach?

DB: A couple of things: One, I was looking for a filter to use in analyzing opportunities that present themselves almost on a daily basis, to determine what was worthy of our time and interest, so that we would not be spending our time and resources on ideas that really did not contribute to the overall fit and success of our organization. So, it provided a rational way for us to do that. Two, it utilized a broad range of component parts that come together for you to determine the ideal driving force of the company. I thought their concept of driving force was very interesting.

DPI: It helped crystallize your thinking about your business's driving force?

DB: Correct. That wasn't too obvious to me or to any of our senior managers, all of whom had different ideas as to what drives our business. Now we have gone through this process, determined what our driving force is, and everybody understands it a lot better. Through the process I am able to understand what is in their minds about our organization, and they, about what is in my mind. Communication was a very positive by-product of the process itself.

I was confused the first day of the three-day session. By the end of the three days, though, I think we had really come together. There was a catharsis that occurred. It had boiled down to three possible driving forces, all of which had some attractiveness. In exploring the potential of each possible driving force, the process takes you through the ultimate result of each one. By the end, we all felt that we had landed on a driving force that we all could buy into.

DPI: You all achieved consensus?

DB: Yes—perhaps not 100 percent, because it required some of the folks to abandon concepts that they held near and dear to their hearts. It was difficult for some to abandon those and accept this new concept. We ended up with about 12 critical issues that we felt were really central to the success of our organization, and even two years later now, that list is still valid. We've tested it out again this year with some modifications because we've achieved a few of those things, and we still feel good about it. That continues to be the focus for our planning and long-term objectives.

DPI: What changes in your organization, or results, have you seen?

DB: The first thing is that [the Strategic Thinking Process] has given management some commonality of language—commonality of thought. It has provided a new base from which to discuss opportunities, and this filter that I mentioned actually does work where the first question that we ask now is: "Does it help support our critical issues?" And if it doesn't, we just don't do it. We just say, "That's a neat opportunity for somebody, but not for us. We're not going to spend our time on it." We use *our strategy* as a benchmark. It has become part of our thinking process here with our senior managers. For me, being a new CEO at that time, it was helpful for me to know that people who worked for me had gone through this process together and that they shared with me what was concluded. So, I feel a lot more comfortable that we are all rowing this boat in the same direction.

DPI: Has it had a concrete business effect?

DB: Our last fiscal year was very successful, and we felt that some of the things that we initiated as the result of the Strategic Thinking Process were contributing directly to that success. Whether or not I could come up with an actual dollar amount...there is no question in my mind that it contributed to our success last year. The problem in the hospital business is that we are seeing such wide fluctuations in our markets. We've got various regulations affecting how people utilize health services. Medicare has changed their regulations in the last four or five years and continually modify those. Also, other third-party insurers are designing plans that *direct* patients, giving an incentive for a certain kind of behavior, and that is basically beyond our control. So, we can follow our plans to the T and something else outside of that can impact on our business.

It's part of the environment we work with. We see such wide fluctuations in our volumes, and that is what this business is all about. We're capacity driven. So, the shift from in-patient to out-patient work is continuing. As far as strategic direction is concerned, we've used our critical issues as kind of a map as to where we're headed.

DPI: Why did you choose DPI—consultants who are not specifically from the health care industry?

DB: As far as I was concerned I was turned on by the process. And I thought DPI's experience in business actually would assist us in our own strategic thinking process. DPI really relates to the business side and its focus is on assisting you in becoming a more successful organization from a business standpoint. A lot of what happened to us since the change to cost-controlled reimbursement for Medicare is that it has become a competitive arena. So, I saw that as a plus.

Experience with other industries has a bearing on what is going on in the health care industry right now. The DPI consultant did not come with the answers to business problems. We have the answers. We are the experts in health care—he's not. But, he's the expert in helping think through these issues.

I think DPI's Strategic Thinking Process has been a very, very successful thing because I think without it, we'd be going off in all kinds of different directions and not having any idea what we ought to be into, and what we ought not to be into. I've been very pleased with the whole engagement.

Wendell M. Smith, President and CEO, Baldwin Technology Company Inc.

DPI: Let's start with some background on Baldwin's business. What is your business concept?

WS: Baldwin is a business focused very sharply on the special field of control and accessory equipment for the printing industry. We have 110 different products that help a printer to achieve quality, reduce waste, or eliminate messy jobs. The business was started some 70 years ago when William Gegenheimer invented the press washer, which is a device to clean the ink rollers of the press. They are still in use today, and we make three or four thousand of them each year around the world. Our largest selling product now is an automatic blanket cleaner, which cleans the blanket cylinders of the press automatically, so you can keep the printing press running as the cylinders are cleaned. A printer can reduce its waste dramatically and keep productivity up because the automatic cycle for cleaning the cylinders occurs every 20 to 60 minutes. A modern high-speed offset press may cost $5 million. To stop it for 15 minutes every hour to hand-clean the blankets is an expensive operation.

DPI: You have consistently grown well above your industry average. How have you done that?

WS: We've grown about 50 percent by acquisition and 50 percent by internal new developments. We've been able to balance, if you will, the ability to acquire companies and integrate them, and the ability to develop and invent new products, which is so important. We've had this balanced growth posture for a long time.

DPI: As what DPI calls a user class–driven company, in your case serving the press room needs of printers, how have your acquisitions supported your strategy?

WS: Our acquisitions have been quite specific, filling in and broadening the product line to the same customer. In the last two years, acquisitions have accelerated, at least in size. Our first was completed in 1969. Since then, we have made 16 different company or product line acquisitions. There were few acquisitions between 1982 and 1987, and the most recent one under the name of Misomex is a $50 million company. I didn't think, then, that we'd ever be at more than $20 million, much less acquire someone else at $50 million!

Incidentally, I left the company in 1980 and came back in 1984. And that has something to do with why we used the DPI process. In 1984, I came back because the company had the first loss they'd ever seen in their history—not much—but they lost a little money and I was able, happily, to bring together a friendly management-led buyout in 1985.

DPI: What prompted you to bring in DPI for the Strategic Thinking Process?

WS: The concept of driving force was something that (through my mentor Harold Gegenheimer) we had a natural understanding of, and it seemed to me to be the thing we had lost during my absence in 1980 to 1984. I was contemplating long-range planning with the newly formed board. The board felt there ought to be a long-range planning process. To some extent, I wanted to be sure that it was not done in the older traditional style, if I may call it that. We had a fairly loose kind of long-range planning process before I left, and it was later instituted in a very formal and traditional style—a five-year plan—in my absence. And when I came back, I didn't want to propagate the traditional five-year plan book that had been written and wasn't, in my opinion, doing much of value. But I wanted to find a way to get together with the management group.

There is another key factor. We're a decentralized kind of business. With 16 business units, each operating very independently with its own president and every one headed by a national born in his own country or state, you know we all think a little differently. I didn't think that Baldwin was floundering and needed focus so much as it seemed that the Strategic Thinking Process was the best way to get management together and to rethink and remind ourselves of certain key issues. The DPI Strategic Thinking approach struck me as a better process than traditional long-range planning.

DPI: Why is this approach more useful for you and the other Baldwin management people?

WS: I think we've probably spoken about it—the definition of the driving force and the value of a common understanding by the management team, especially in a decentralized situation. They all are running their own lives pretty completely, and so there are moments when people wish to look outside, either for variety or whatever, to other fields. Occasionally, somebody in the management team might look toward trying to apply our technologies to some other totally different market. It may look very attractive at the moment when somebody tells you that you could use that device in the auto parts cleaning industry, for example. And, you know, you look at it and say, "You're darn right, the technology is not very special to printing. Let's proceed and try it out." This is a dangerous step, and through the Strategic Thinking Process we reminded ourselves very strongly once again that we didn't want to divert our attention even though there might be a highly profitable opportunity. In reality, we are turning away from profitable opportunities every day, and to turn away from one more is not going to ruin the company. We've been able to grow much faster than most companies and probably as fast as we can control well without going to other fields.

I think the process, particularly as we've gotten bigger, with more people involved, increases management's understanding. You're taking the whole group and reminding yourselves of what it is that has worked throughout this time period, and that focus is very important to our success. I could probably have relayed that kind of thinking to that same group by other means, but not as successfully or in the same condensed time frame.

13

The Logistics of the Strategic Thinking Process

Strategic Thinking is the *process* used by a leader to formulate, articulate, communicate, and implement a clear, concise, and explicit strategy and vision for his or her organization. Unfortunately, in many organizations the strategy of the company is not always clear. It usually resides in the head of the chief executive exclusively. Other people around the CEO have to guess at what the strategy is. Because they have not been involved in the process, or because the CEO cannot clearly articulate the strategy, they feel no commitment to, or ownership of, that vision. Our own experience shows that most managers are so engrossed in operational activity that they have not developed the skills to *think strategically*. A CEO, therefore, might wish to involve his or her subordinates in a deliberate strategic process for strictly educational value. The problem, however, is that most CEOs practice this process by osmosis and are not conscious of its

Portions of this chapter have been excerpted from the author's two previous publications, *The Strategist CEO* (copyright 1988 by Michel Robert) and *The Essence of Leadership* (copyright 1991 by Michel Robert). Both books are published by Quorum Books, an imprint of Greenwood Publishing Group, Inc., Westport, Conn.

various steps. It is usually impossible to transfer to anyone else a skill that one cannot describe.

The Role of the CEO as Process Owner

There is only one person in any organization who can "drive" the strategic thinking process and that is the chief executive of the organization. Strategic Thinking must start at the top of the organization. Strategic Thinking is definitely a "trickle down" process and not a "bubble up" one. It is a very interactive process, but the CEO must be its owner. As such, the CEO must show commitment to the process by participating in all of its steps.

Because the process is highly interactive, it is not for the faint of heart. The process invites discussion, debate, and constructive provocation. Everyone, during the process, has the opportunity to express his or her views, have these challenged, and then challenge those of others. As a result, the process is ideal for CEOs who encourage frank, open discussion of issues and challenges. CEOs who are not comfortable with this type of management style should not use our approach.

The Strategic Thinking Process leads to better implementation of the strategy. In our experience, there are only two ways to implement one's strategy—by *compliance* or by *commitment.*

Compliance is having the CEO tell his or her subordinates what the strategy is and how it is expected to be executed. The CEO then farms out different tasks to each subordinate. They, in turn, implement without questioning its rationale. In this world of increasing complexity, we have found that this approach is having less and less appeal.

The second, and more effective method, is through *commitment.* Commitment comes by active participation in the rationale behind the strategy. As a result, we recommend that all key "stakeholders" be involved in each step of the process.

One role that the CEO should not attempt to play is that of process facilitator. One cannot have a foot in the process and another foot in the content. Attempting to guide the process while participating in the debate will give everyone the impression that the

CEO is trying to manipulate the process to a predetermined conclusion. Therefore, it is wise to have an outside third party guide the process along.

The Role of the Process Facilitator

Many CEOs have attempted to use our process by playing the role of owner and facilitator only to call us quickly after their first meeting. Each would then recite to us the difficulties mentioned in the previous paragraph.

Whenever a client hires us to assist in the strategy effort of the company, he or she wants to take several hours to indoctrinate us in the details of the business. After a few minutes, I diplomatically ask the client to stop. It is not an advantage to know the client's business in depth. In fact, it is a disadvantage. I tell my clients that getting to know their business too well might make us lose our objectivity because we might start to empathize with their problems. There are several pragmatic roles that a trained third-party facilitator can play.

First, a few thoughts on the word *facilitator*. Facilitators are not moderators. A moderator is a person who directs traffic as best as he or she can during a meeting but without the use of any specific process. A process facilitator has a very different role. This is a person who comes to the meeting with a structured process together with specific instruments that keep the discussion moving forward in a constructive manner. The facilitator also keeps the process honest, balanced, and objective. The CEO of a *Fortune* 10 company used to say to this author: "You know Mike, you're the only one in this room who can tell me to sit down and I do. Nobody else in this room would dare say that!"

The question of using external or internal resources as facilitators of the process is an important one and usually comes up in all large companies with whom we work.

Normally, most clients will ask us to facilitate the initial interventions. As the desire to cascade the process down the organization increases, it makes sense for the client to use internal resources. One part of our service, then, is to train these internal

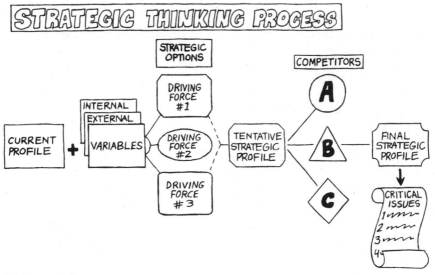

Figure 13-1.

facilitators and equip them to continue the effort within their respective units. There are a number of good reasons to do this:

- The client takes ownership of the process.
- Internal facilitators can assist in the management of critical issues.
- Internal facilitators can tailor the instruments to unique or different situations.
- Internal facilitators can assist with the integration of the operational and strategic plans into the strategic profile.

The Process

Our Strategic Thinking Process incorporates eight steps (Figure 13-1). These are:

1. Clarification of the current profile
2. Analysis of strategic variables
3. Exploration of different driving forces and possible strategic profiles (strategic options)

4. Development of a tentative future strategic profile
5. Development of competitive profiles
6. Anticipation of the implications of your strategy
7. Final strategic profile
8. Identification of critical issues

Clarification of the Current Profile

The first step in the process is taking stock of where the organization currently is. To do this one needs to take a "photograph" of the organization in its present state. One cannot have an intelligent discussion as to "what we want to be" unless we clearly understand "what we look like today." Therefore, one needs to know:

- The scope of current products and services
- How these products or services are grouped
- The trends or cycles they experience
- The scope of the geographic areas they serve
- The user groups they have attracted
- The growth of these groups in the last few years
- Their market share and that of the competition
- The organizational structure in place to support the identified product/market division
- The return of each product/market division
- The organization's current *driving force*
- The organization's current *business concept*
- The organization's current *areas of excellence*

Collection of this information provides management with a "snapshot" or current profile of the organization (Figure 13-2).

```
CURRENT
PROFILE
```

Figure 13-2.

Figure 13-3.

This is the composition of the organization as it is presently being propelled by a certain driving force.

Analysis of Strategic Variables

Any sound strategy must allow the organization to successfully deal with its environment. Thus, the second step in strategic thinking is an analysis of the strategic variables that will be working for or against the business in the future (Figure 13-3). These variables, however, usually reside inside the heads of the management team and must be extracted and debated in a structured and objective forum with an outside person facilitating the process.

These variables are usually highly subjective in nature and are each person's view of what may or may not occur inside—but more importantly, outside—the organization. These differing views must be discussed in a rational manner in order for everyone involved to agree on the most important factors that the business will have to face.

The old saying "garbage in, garbage out" is very applicable in strategic thinking. The quality of the strategic inputs determines to a great extent the quality of the outcome of such an exercise. However, in order to obtain high-quality inputs, there is no need to undertake massive and costly studies about the future and its negative predictions. The best inputs are stored in the minds of the key people who run the company. Future direction is greatly influenced by the experience and perceptions of these people about the internal and external environment in which the organization exists. The trick is to tap this wealth of knowledge and bring it forward in an objective forum.

To do this we have developed a strategic input survey that *each* member of management answers. The survey obtains everyone's view on 11 key areas of the internal and external environment.

Internal Environment

Products
- The common characteristics of products or services
- The exceptionally successful products
- The characteristics of their success
- The exceptionally unsuccessful products
- The characteristics of their failure

Geographic Markets
- The common characteristics of geographic markets
- The exceptionally successful geographic markets
- The characteristics of their success
- The exceptionally unsuccessful markets
- The characteristics of their failure

User Segments
- The common characteristics of user segments
- The exceptionally successful user segments
- The characteristics of their success
- The exceptionally unsuccessful user segments
- The characteristics of their failure

Corporate Beliefs
- The principles, beliefs, and values that guide corporate behavior

Strengths
- The *unique* strengths of the organization
- The strengths possessed to a greater extent by the organization than by the competition
- Traits that may become strengths later

Weaknesses
- The *unique* weaknesses of the organization
- The weaknesses possessed to a greater extent by the organization than by the competition
- Traits that may become weaknesses later

Internal Opportunities
- Short-term internal opportunities
- Medium-term internal opportunities
- Long-term internal opportunities

External Environment

Competition
- Direct competitors (present and future)
- Indirect competitors (present and future)
- Their strengths
- Their weaknesses
- New forms of competition
- Suppliers or customers that may become competitors

Opportunities/Threats
- Short-term external opportunities/threats
- Medium-term external opportunities/threats
- Long-term external opportunities/threats

Strategic Vulnerability Areas
- Raw materials
- Technology
- Labor
- Legislation
- Capital

Using the preceding categories, our strategic input survey consists of 42 key questions that are asked of each member of the management team. Their answers to these questions are all the data required as a basis for the development of a strategic profile for the organization. The consolidation of the information extracted from each person is the best environmental "scan" one can do. As mentioned before, this information is highly qualitative in nature; nevertheless, it is the foundation of sound strategic thinking.

Explore Different Strategic Scenarios

Exploration of Different Driving Forces and Possible Strategic Profiles

Once the management team have agreed to the variables that will work for or against the organization in the future, they can explore which components of the business can best be leveraged in the company's favor and around which a successful strategy can be developed (Figure 13-4). There are usually two or three areas of the business around which a strategy can be formulated. No company has access to all ten driving forces, but most have access to two or three. And most companies, over time, have built up capabilities in two or three areas of the business that can serve as the root of a future strategy.

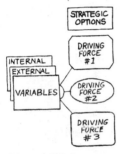

Figure 13-4.

It now becomes important for management to clearly understand what the two or three areas are and then to draw "profiles" as to where each one would lead the organization and what the organization would "look" like if that avenue were pursued. Each area requires emphasis or de-emphasis on different products, customers, market segments, and geographic areas so that each picture will turn out to be "different." At this junction, management can make a choice as to which pictures they like better and wish to embark upon.

Determine the Business's Future Strategic Heartbeat. Once management have agreed (and it's not an easy task) on what is currently driving the business, they need to consider these questions: What *should drive* the business in the future? Should we continue to be driven as we have been, or should we explore another driving force? If so, which one should that be? What implications will that have on the choices we make on the nature of products, customers, and markets we currently offer or do not offer? What will we end up "looking" like as an organization if we change the driving force of our company?

The management team can then identify which component of the business is *strategically* more important to the organization's survival and is the *key determinant* of the company's products, markets, and customers. In other words, which part of the business is at the root of the organization and can be leveraged by the company as its strategic weapon against its environment in the future?

Develop a Coherent Strategy and Business Concept. It is now imperative to develop a statement of strategy, which can be communicated to those who will be called upon to carry it out, around the element of the business that will drive the organization forward. The statement needs to be articulated in terms precise and concise enough so that people can carry it around in their heads. It should represent the *conceptual underpinning* of the organization and its *raison d'être.*

Translate the Strategy into a Strategic Profile and Vision. The next step is to translate the strategy into a "vision" of what the business will look like sometime "down the road." This vision should be a description of the products, customers, market segments, and geographic markets that the organization will emphasize and deemphasize in the future. This vision or "profile" then serves everyone as a "test bed" for the allocation of resources and the types of opportunities that are to be pursued in the future.

A strategic profile should be short enough that it can be carried around in one's head, and the boundaries should be clear and precise enough that managers can use it daily as a test bed for their decisions. Like picture painters, the master strategist must know what to include in the strategic profile. The following section describes the items that need to be clearly articulated.

Development of a Future Strategic Profile

Time Frame. A suitable time period for strategic thinking needs to be agreed upon. There is no rule, and it should be determined by the nature of the business.

Driving Force and Business Concept. The driving force that will propel the organization should be clearly established. This should be accompanied by a short description of the business concept that will be pursued in this mode. Because it is possible for two competitors within the same industry to have the same driving force but different business concepts, the particular description each one attaches to the driving force may influence greatly the direction it pursues. Volkswagen and Daimler-Benz, for example, are both product-driven companies. However, the definition that each gives to its product leads the two automobile companies down different paths in everything they do, including product design, pricing, advertising, distribution, and manufacturing. BMW and Porsche describe their "product" in yet a slightly different manner, which gives each company its own uniqueness and separates them from either Daimler-Benz or Volkswagen.

The description of the driving force is the description of the singular business concept or purpose of the organization. It is the conceptual underpinning of the business that sets the parameters for the scope of products, geographic markets, and user segments.

Although corporations may get very large, the original idea that got them started is usually very simple and can be described in one or two sentences. It needs to be clear and crisp so that it can easily be retained by the dozens, hundreds, or thousands of people who are called upon to perpetuate it.

Akio Morita's concept of "using electronic technology in ingenious ways" is a good example of a technology-driven business concept that was at the root of Mr. Morita's vision and has been propelling Sony ever since.

CEOs who have difficulty articulating and disseminating their business concept will have great difficulty getting their key executives' commitment to any one direction. Furthermore, the inability to clearly define and articulate the business concept leads to the failure to establish an "edge" in the marketplace.

Areas of Excellence. The next elements to clearly establish are those two or three activities within the company that require excellence to a greater degree than any competitor has achieved, or to a greater degree than anything else the company does, if the business concept is to maintain its strength. Every organization excels in two or three areas, and it is this excellence that gives the business concept its strength. For a business concept to maintain its strength in the future, the areas of excellence that fuel this strength need to be identified and cultivated.

A product-driven company, for example, will need to excel at product development in order to improve current products and develop new ones. These skills are normally accompanied by excellent selling skills in order to convince more and more clients to buy the products. The areas of excellence vary from one driving force to another. Knowing which one is to be perfected will determine how resources are allocated.

Product Scope. Management must now turn its attention to listing the type of current and future products that are suited to this business concept and that will receive *more* emphasis in the future. They must also list those current and future products that are *not* suited to the business concept and will therefore receive *less* emphasis. This short list will serve as a filter for future product opportunities and test for a "fit." A product that falls on the less emphasis side should serve as a red flag to the company, telling it that the company is not organized to support this type of product opportunity, and it should not be pursued.

Market/User Scope. The same is done for geographic markets and user groups. In each instance, management will draw a list identifying those markets/groups that will be pursued and those that will not. Again, the objective is to construct a screen for future market or user opportunities.

Size/Growth Guidelines. The next part of the profile is to clarify the size and growth guidelines that the organization should achieve during the strategic time frame. The key word here is *guidelines*.

These are usually ranges of numbers in categories such as sales, revenues, turnover, and growth.

Return/Profit Guidelines. The return/profit category specifies numbers that reflect guidelines for profit and return. The size/growth, return/profit guidelines should be representative of the financial performance required to provide the necessary cash flow to enable the organization to achieve its strategic profile.

Corporate Beliefs. One executive described corporate beliefs as "moral guidelines, written or unwritten, that a company sets for itself in dealing with its environment." Although corporate beliefs are not part of the strategic profile of an organization, they are integral to the strategic thinking of the organization's leaders. The values, beliefs, and principles that these people own go a long way toward setting the tone of corporate behavior and molding the scope of its products and markets. They are to the strategic profile what the frame is to a painting.

Corporate beliefs exist in every company even though they are not always visible or known. However, once they have been drawn out of top management, our recommendation is always that they accompany any publication of the strategic profile, because they are the moral foundation upon which the company is based.

To illustrate their importance, two examples come to mind. We once worked with a tobacco manufacturer who, during one of our sessions, identified as an opportunity the possibility of obtaining distribution in one of the largest department store chains. Because this chain did not carry tobacco products, distribution alone would have meant a sizable initial order and a chance to significantly increase market share. The company set about devising an elaborate plan to approach the chain's buyer. By coincidence, we had also worked with the department store and knew that this possibility would never materialize. We informed the tobacco manufacturer of our opinion. "Why?" he asked. The reason was simple. The founder of the department store chain was a devout abstainer, and no tobacco or alcoholic products would ever be offered for sale in his stores. His personal belief, then and now, dictates corporate behavior.

The second example occurred when I was with Johnson & Johnson in the 1960s. Baby oil is one of its products, and the company started noticing that teenagers and adults used it every spring as a suntanning lotion. It works well when used this way because baby oil has no sunscreening ingredient. We saw an opportunity, and every spring Johnson & Johnson started promoting its baby oil in the suntan market. It was so successful that within a few years J&J had the market's largest share. At the same time, however, there was emerging research indicating that overexposure to the sun might be a possible cause of skin cancer. J&J—at that time and still now—had a corporate belief that said it would "never offer for sale any product that may prove to be a hazard to a person's health." The suntan market experience was violating this belief. A decision was made in 1969 to withdraw all promotional funds and activities from the suntanning market with a resultant loss of 15 percent in baby oil sales.

These corporate beliefs, known as the Credo, existed then and still dictate J&J's corporate behavior today. *Fortune* magazine once did a story on J&J, and a large segment of the article was naturally devoted to "The General's Credo."

The force that holds J&J together is an improbable one—the Credo, a 291-word code of corporate behavior that has a mystical but nonetheless palpable influence in the company. The Credo is a legacy of "the General," Robert Wood Johnson, the son of one of the founding Johnson brothers and the man who, during his long rule from 1938 to 1963, shaped the company. Rare is the conversation with a J&J executive in which the Credo does not come up. Several years ago, company officers debated for hours before changing a paragraph in the document. When one looks at the scope of J&J products and markets, one can look to the Credo as a key filter to the choices this company has made in the areas of its strategic profile.

Some outsiders might consider the Credo not so much corny, as wrong-headed: It commands that the company service customers first (especially mothers, nurses, doctors, and patients), employees second, the communities in which the company operates third, and the shareholders last. J&J has sometimes sacrificed earnings in what is perceived to be the best interest of the customers. Its behavior in the Chicago Tylenol case is a good example of adherence to this Credo.

Development of Competitive Profiles

As outsiders, it is still surprisingly easy to determine the driving force of an organization's key competitors (Figure 13-5). One only needs to look at their actions in the marketplace. By knowing their driving force, one can then anticipate what they will do in the future. We were working with a film manufacturer not too long ago and it identified that one of its major competitors was production capacity–driven. In a soft market, such an organization usually resorts to price cutting in order to maintain volumes. Our client anticipated this type of behavior from that one competitor and, sure enough, a week later that is exactly what the competitor did. This time, however, our client was ready, and the competitor's action had little effect.

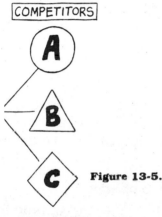

Figure 13-5.

Next in the Strategic Thinking Process is the construction of future profiles for the organization's three or four major competitors. By identifying each competitor's driving force, one can easily anticipate which products, markets, and user groups it will pursue and which ones it won't. These profiles will be valuable to have in order to proceed to the next step—the test step.

Anticipation of the Implications of Your Strategy

Often, when chief executives change the strategy and direction of their organization, they do not take time to think through the *im-*

plications of that change. As a result, they end up reacting to these changes as they "bump" into them. Every change in strategy— even a minor one—will bring implications of one kind or another. If you want your strategy to succeed, you must devote some time and thought to identifying the issues that stand in the way of making your strategy work. What are all the changes that need to be addressed in order for the strategy to work? These changes become what we, at DPI, call *strategic critical issues.* These issues become management's agenda; each is assigned to a specific person who becomes the "owner" of the issue and who is held responsible and accountable to get the issue resolved. My friends at 3M call this "pin the rose" time. It is the successful management and resolution of these issues that will ensure the implementation of the strategy.

The test of the future strategic profile has three parts:

1. Versus the current profile
2. Versus the strategic inputs
3. Versus the competitive profiles

Versus the Current Profile. This test consists of comparing the future strategic profile to the current profile (Figure 13-6). The type of questions asked are:

- How large are the gaps between the two profiles?
- What changes need to be made to go from the current product scope to the new product scope?
- What changes need to be made to go from the current market scope to the new market scope?
- What changes need to be made to go from the current user groups to the new user groups?

Figure 13-6.

- What new resources/skills will be required?
- Is it realistic to achieve this within this time frame?
- How should the strategy and profile be modified in view of the preceding?

Versus the Strategic Inputs. This test consists of comparing the future strategic profile to the original strategic inputs about the external and internal environment (Figure 13-7). The questions asked are:

- Are the organization's unique strengths being exploited?
- Are its unique weaknesses being minimized?
- Are any corporate beliefs being violated?
- Are all major opportunities being exploited?
- Are all major threats being avoided?
- How should the profile be modified?

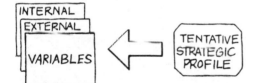

Figure 13-7.

Versus the Competitive Profiles. This test consists of comparing the future strategic profile to each of the major competitors that will be attracted to your strategy (Figure 13-8). The questions asked are:

- Is our strategy running up against their strengths?
- Are their weaknesses being exploited?
- How will they react to this strategy?
- How can their actions be counteracted?
- What is driving their strategy?
- How can we offset their areas of excellence?

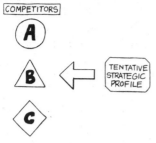

Figure 13-8.

Final Strategic Profile

The three-part test just completed brings to the surface a number of issues and provides an opportunity to try to "shoot holes" in management's thinking (Figure 13-9). It also affords management the chance to reshape the organization's strategy and profile one more time before adopting it.

Figure 13-9.

Identification of Critical Issues

Determining the final strategic profile will also bring to the surface a number of key issues that management will need to resolve if the organization's future strategic profile is to become a reality (Figure 13-10). These critical issues are the bridge between the current profile and the final strategic profile (Figure 13-11). Setting the direction of the organization has been achieved. Now managing that direction starts, and managing that direction on an ongoing basis means the ongoing management of the critical issues.

Structure. There was a fad in the 1970s and 1980s to reorganize and restructure companies. After the reorganization, the question

Figure 13-10.

Figure 13-11. *(Copyright ©1989 by Decision Processes International. All rights reserved.)*

that was heard was: "Now that we are reorganized, where are we going?"

In our view, structure follows strategy. The organization structure of the business must be in support of the direction of that business. We have further learned that each driving force requires a slightly different organization structure. A product concept–driven company does not organize like a customer class–driven company.

Figures 13-12 to 13-15 are examples of organization charts for a few of the driving forces defined in Chapter 4.

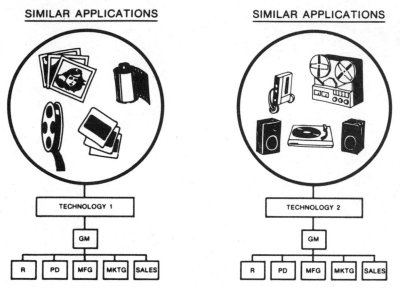

Figure 13-12. Technology-driven organization.

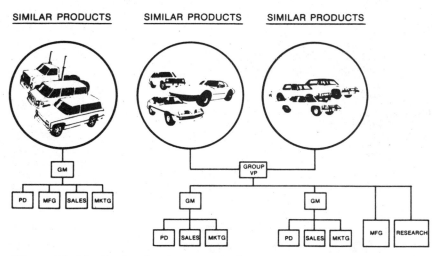

Figure 13-13. Product/service concept–driven organization.

Systems. The next discussion that leads to critical issues is one that revolves around the subject of "systems." Many companies today have purchased sophisticated and costly electronic information systems only to find out sometime later that the systems are not sup-

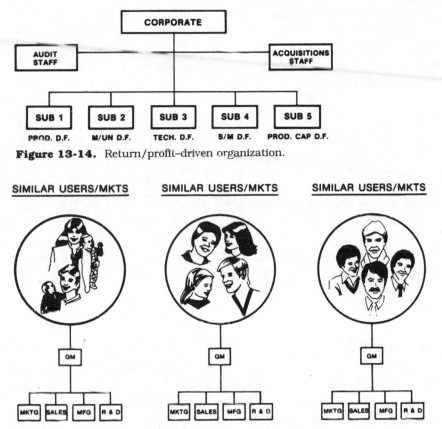

Figure 13-14. Return/profit–driven organization.

Figure 13-15. User/market class–driven organization.

portive of the company's business strategy. Again, our view is that all information systems must be aligned with the direction of the organization and that there are usually critical issues that surface in this area of systems.

Skills. When an organization changes its direction, this change will usually require the acquisition of a new set of skills. These can be developed, but frequently they do not reside in-house and must be acquired, thus giving rise to another set of critical issues.

Compensation. In spite of all the titles or power you might think you have over people, my experience has convinced me that *people do not do what you want them to do; people do what they are paid to do.* If your strategy says that you want your people to behave in a certain manner, but your compensation system rewards them to do something different, I can bet you anything that at the end of the year they will have done what they were paid to do and not what you wanted them to do.

As a result, another area of discussion that raises critical issues is one around the subject of compensation to identify changes that need to be made to assure that the compensation of key individuals is geared to support the strategy and direction of the business.

Summary. Around these four areas—structure, systems, skills, and compensation—a number of critical issues are identified and assigned to specific individuals for resolution. The results expected are articulated, the macro action steps are listed, other people that need to be involved are assigned to each team, and completion and review dates are established.

The Results

We have noticed a variety of different results from the use of the Strategic Thinking Process, and we make a point of asking each of our clients what value they received. Without exception, six items are always mentioned: clarity, focus, consensus, cohesion, commitment, and filter.

Clarity

Although not every client changes its direction as a result of this exercise, all clients have said that the process brought clarity to their strategic thinking. As a group, the management team starts the process with slightly different perceptions of the company's strategy or, in some instances, with a nonarticulated and somewhat fuzzy strategy. At the end of the exercise, however, the team has produced a crystal-clear strategic profile. Each member of the management team now shares only *one* vision of the organization's future.

The profile can also be used to bring clarity to other people in the organization. Some of our clients have published all or parts of the strategic profile to communicate the company's strategy to various interested groups—for example, in annual reports to inform shareholders of the company's direction. Others have used it as a discussion piece in internal forums with employees. Corporate beliefs usually get published extensively. As the driving force is the *heart* of strategic thinking, corporate beliefs are its soul.

Focus

Focus is another output of the process. The strategic profile produces a better tool to allocate resources and to manage the time and efforts of others. It enables them to direct their efforts toward activities that complement the desired direction of the company and to avoid wasted efforts on nonrelated issues.

When we asked the chief executive of Alcan why the metal tent card with the inscription "Our product is aluminum" faces the visitor to his office, he replied, "I don't want any of our people talking to me about any other subject than aluminum." The metal used for the tent card is, of course, aluminum.

Consensus

The process brings about consensus at each step. The debates and discussions are conducted in such a manner that agreement is achieved *systematically* on each key issue before moving on the next one. The assignments worked on during the work session are designed to place on the table all the key questions about the future of the organization. These instruments bring forward everyone's best thinking and provide an opportunity for each person to present his or her views, opinions, and rationale on every important issue. We have found that it is not sufficient only to collect a person's perceptions through a survey, but that a person needs an opportunity to explain and elaborate his or her point of view.

A group vice president said of his superior, the sector vice president, at the end of one of our work sessions: "I have worked with this man for over 20 years. Yet, I found out more about his views on our business in the last three days." This expression has been heard in many of the strategy sessions with which we have been involved.

Because the process provides a forum to discuss issues in an orderly manner, there is never a dissenting voice at the end of the work session. This unquestionably contributes to a more harmonious organization.

Cohesion

"Hockey-stick planning," one executive told us, "leads to hockey-puck management." Without a clear strategic profile the organization bounces from one seemingly good idea to another. It zigzags its way forward and expends valuable time, money, and effort leapfrogging from one suspicious opportunity to another. When there is no clear direction accompanied by a solid test bed to screen opportunities, management can often be seduced by the financial aspects of an opportunity only to discover later that there is no fit with the rest of the organization's activities. The strategic profile becomes the bedrock or cornerstone of their actions and, when used in such a manner, results in a synchronization of resources instead of dispersion and fragmentation. Less time will be wasted exploring undesired options and less effort will be expended justifying the existence of the "sunset" portions of the business.

Commitment

At the end of the process there is absolute commitment from all management team members to the new direction. The reason is simple: It is *their* strategy. They participated at every step. All their views were heard and their inputs considered. This commitment sometimes comes from surprising quarters. The vice president of a division of a complex multinational, whose unit was going to be de-emphasized in the future, said to us, "I recognize the fact that we're not going to be getting the same resources as in the past, but I'm totally committed to that decision. I now understand why those funds need to be given to other parts of the business." This is an important achievement. Every organization must discriminate between its various units when allocating resources, and it is important that the managers of the less fortunate units understand the reasons. These units still need to be managed well even though they may not be the "stars" of the future. In this instance, our process served as a unifying force within the organization.

"For any strategy to succeed, you need operating people to *understand* it, *embrace* it, and *make it happen*," says Roger Schipke, senior vice president of General Electric. We couldn't agree more.

Filter

Probably the best use of the strategic profile is as a filter for the operational plans and new product or market opportunities. As an operational filter, the strategic profile can reduce and even eliminate "hockey-puck" management. It clearly identifies the areas of more emphasis and less emphasis in the future. This knowledge should be "etched" on the brain of every key manager and used as a "working sieve to guide their daily operational decisions and actions." Such was the use a general manager of a client organization wanted his subordinates to make of this tool.

More important, the strategic profile is an excellent way to ferret out good from less promising products or market opportunities. When these opportunities present themselves, the answers to a few questions can quickly test their "fit" with the organization's strategic profile and direction.

- Does this opportunity complement or violate the driving force and business concept?
- Does this opportunity bring products that fit those that will receive more emphasis or less emphasis in the future?
- Does this opportunity bring markets that fit those that will receive more emphasis or less emphasis in the future?
- Does the opportunity bring users that fit those that will receive more emphasis or less emphasis in the future?
- Does this opportunity bring products, markets, and users that can be supported by the present areas of excellence? Or will it require excellence in areas beyond our current capabilities?
- Does this opportunity meet the size/growth, return/profit guidelines?

This quick test can help an organization in two ways.

1. If you receive negative responses to each of these questions, beware—it may be a good financial opportunity but there may not be an appropriate "fit" with what you are currently doing. Experience has shown that there needs to be more reason than money to exploit an opportunity. In our view those other reasons are a fit with the driving force, business concept, areas of excellence, and products market/user scopes.

2. If there is no apparent fit but you still want to pursue the opportunity, it might be better to do so under some other form of organization structure. Your present structure does not support the type of opportunity being considered. Another form might.

The value that a strategic thinking process brings to a company is hard to measure in tangible terms. We have been involved with clients that have made important strategic decisions during the work session which involved substantial sums of money and which had enormous impact on the company. The intangible rewards are much more discrete but probably have as much of an impact. These seem to be of as much value to clients as the more tangible ones.

The process of strategic thinking described in this chapter has been developed and refined while working with client organizations. It is not a theoretical approach to the subject; it is a tested methodology currently being used by a number of corporations. It places, in logical order, the various elements that management needs to consider in order to conduct its strategic thinking in a time-efficient manner. It assembles and collects management's impressions and opinions about the environment in order to conceptualize or synthesize a collective vision to deal with that environment.

Closing the Loop

At this point, you might be wondering how all the concepts presented tie together. Figure 13-16 attempts to link everything discussed previously into a cohesive whole.

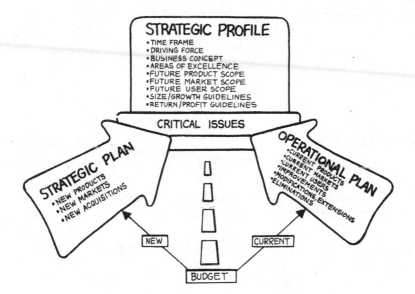

Figure 13-16. Closing the loop.

The rectangle at the top of the graphic represents the output of our Strategic Thinking Process, which we first referred to in Chapter 2. The strategic profile is a description of "what" an organization wants to "look like" at some point in the future. The inside of the rectangle contains the content of this picture. The critical issues are the "bridge" that needs to be crossed in order to go from what the company looks like today to what it wants to look like tomorrow. Now comes planning time.

The Operational Plan

At this point in the process, one needs to examine the organization's current activities and decide which products, customers, and markets need to be improved or modified. Moreover, one must identify those that need to be eliminated because they no longer fit the "vision" of what the company is trying to become.

One of the most difficult decisions we find management having to make is not what to do but rather what not to do anymore. This is so because there is always someone telling management to "hang in" a little longer—that the corner is about to come but, in fact, it never does. During the operational planning stage, these decisions become easier to make because all have agreed that they no longer fit the aspiration of the type of company they are trying to build.

The Strategic Plan

In our view, a strategic plan is one that will alter the look of an organization in the future. Obviously, those elements of the business that are no longer desired meet this definition. The more important elements that will alter the look of a company in the future are the products, customers, and markets that the company wants to add to that look. A plan now needs to be constructed to make this happen.

Our experience shows that if you want to give birth to brand new activities (products, markets, acquisitions), it is wise at the beginning to have people other than those who are running your current businesses midwife these projects. The rationale is simple: Those running your current businesses have a locomotive on their hands, and keeping that engine on track will require all their time and energy. As such, it is wise to have new activities managed outside the normal structure of the current business.

The Strategic Profile Is the Target for All Decisions

As the graphic in Figure 13-16 clearly illustrates, the strategic profile becomes the target for all the decisions that are made in the organization. Plans and decisions that "fit" inside the "frame" of the profile are pursued, and those that do not "fit" are not.

Tool to Allocate Resources

The last piece in this jigsaw is the budget. And, again, the strategic profile is the anchor for these decisions. Management must now ensure that resources are allocated to all plans in order to guarantee their viability.

The Mechanics
of the Process

Before describing *how* we work with the Strategic Thinking Process in a client organization, it is important to say a few words about DPI's role in such an assignment. Our role, as an outside consultant, is *not* to set the direction of the client's organization. We feel quite strongly that no outside consultant can or should attempt to dictate a client's strategy. No outside consultant can ever learn enough about his or her client's business or ever know as much about that business as the people who run it. Nor should a consultant attempt to set the strategy if the consultant is not going to have to live with the results of that strategy.

The role that a consultant can undertake, however, is to *facilitate* the process of strategic thinking. As facilitators, we can keep the forum on track and bring objectivity to the discussions. We do not use the word *facilitator* to mean having someone in the room to take notes. Our meaning is that of a *trained* facilitator following a *predetermined process* and using *predesigned instruments* to ensure that all the necessary questions are raised and debated. A facilitator's role is to place the participants in the appropriate discussion groups in order to tap everyone's knowledge and expertise in an orderly way. It is with this understanding of our role that we can then assist clients to set their own direction following a time-efficient formula that we will now describe.

Phase I: Prework

Each member of the management team answers our two questionnaires, the Current Profile Survey and the Strategic Input Analysis Survey. This work requires three to five hours of effort by each person and is done without consulting one's colleagues. Our objective is to extract each person's best thinking on all the key elements of the business and its environment. The answers are sent to us for editing and collating.

Phase II: Three-Day
Work Session

With the sum of views from the two questionnaires as our major inputs, we now come together to establish a strategy and a *future* strategic profile. During the work session, management discusses all of these inputs in subgroups using predesigned discussion instruments that raise all the necessary questions and activate the debate.

The three days are divided as follows.

Day 1

- We obtain agreement on the current profile and the current driving force.
- We review all the strategic inputs and agree on the two or three most important ones in each category.

Day 2

- We use the abridged strategic inputs from day 1 to choose two or three potential driving forces.
- We develop profiles for each potential driving force and compare them to the current profile.
- We choose a tentative strategic profile.

Day 3

- We develop competitive strategic profiles.
- We test the tentative strategic profile and bring to the surface critical issues. We shape and mold the final strategic profile.

Phase III: One-Day Work Session

After a three-to-four-week break, we reassemble for another day that is dedicated to advancing the process in the following manner:

- Development of strategic objectives
- Development of operational goals

Phase IV: Critical Issues Meeting

There will be two half-day meetings with the CEO and his or her "inner circle" to review progress on the critical issues. At these meetings, the "owners" of the issues will be expected to report progress.

Phase V: Two-Day Review

Some 8 to 10 months after the first work session, we reconvene as a group to revisit our strategy. Because the conclusions of the first three-day session were reached on the basis of assumptions that were made about what might or might not occur in the environment, we now need to reassess those assumptions. This reassessment will also allow us to fine-tune our strategic position and bring to the surface any new critical issues.

During this process, the facilitator compiles, edits, collates, and produces all discussion papers and final reports.

"Three days to set the direction of an organization is not enough time," some people will say. Our answer to that is, "That is true when you don't have a process." Without a process, executives can literally spend months and sometimes years trying to get agreement as to the future direction of the organization. This happens because the lack of methodology forces strategy formulation to be done on-the-run and in a haphazard way. With a good process, three days is more than ample time, as we've proven in a large number of client organizations.

Many of the systems that we have seen used in companies are overly complex and time-consuming. Too frequently they end up producing volumes of paper that are shelved together with the pictures and the awards.

Our process produces a strategic profile that a person can remember easily and practice daily. When transcribed to paper, it should not be more than two or three pages in length. The most successful organizations are those that keep things simple and do a few things extremely well. The same is true of strategic thinking.

Summary

Strategic thinking is, to us, the most important skill required of a chief executive and leader of an organization. Followers, generally, do not follow leaders blindly, and unless the leader can articulate his or her vision and get the commitment of followers to that vision, he or she will be forging ahead alone.

In a book called *The Leader-Manager* (Baltelle Press, 1991), Dr. William D. Hilt conducted a survey to identify some common characteristics of leaders across cultures and organizations. From his study, he concluded that four basic traits appeared in all leaders, irrespective of organization or country.

1. The leader had a clear vision for the organization.
2. The leader had the ability to communicate this vision to others.
3. The leader had the ability to motivate others to work toward this vision.
4. The leader had the ability to "work the system" to get things done.

Although we agree with these four characteristics, our experience shows that leaders have great difficulty articulating their strategy and vision to others. Thus, it becomes imperative for the leader to clearly understand the process of strategic thinking in order to involve others in the development of the strategy. This is how motivation, commitment, and successful implementation result.

Is the Stock Market an Obstacle to Strategic Decision Making?

For years, U.S. managers have been urged to make investments that improve the long-run competitiveness of their firms. Advocates of this view frequently point to examples of Japanese managers deliberately sacrificing short-term profits to gain substantial market shares for their firms. Many U.S. managers, however, argue that it is difficult to adopt a long-run perspective in today's business environment. The biggest obstacle to long-run or strategic decision making, they claim, is the stock market. For example, in a survey of 100 CEOs of major corporations, 89 agreed that the competitive edge of the United States has been dulled by failure to emphasize long-term investment. Ninety-two

This appendix is reprinted with permission of J. Randall Woolridge and Charles C. Snow, Pennsylvania University.

percent of this group believed that Wall Street's preoccupation with quarterly earnings was the cause.

Are U.S. managers forced to manage for the short term in order to meet the demands of Wall Street? The answer, quite simply, is no. The study that provided the basis for this conclusion examined 767 investment decisions made by 248 companies in 102 industries and announced in the *Wall Street Journal*. The results of this study show that the stock market usually reacts positively (in the form of excess stock returns) to corporate announcements of strategic investments decisions. This finding holds for investments that are large or small and of short or long duration.

Hypotheses about the Stock Market

According to traditional valuation theory, the market value of a firm is the sum of the discounted value of future cashflows expected to be generated from assets in place and the net present value of expected cashflows from investment opportunities that are expected to be available to and undertaken by the firm in the future. The value of a firm changes as the stock market receives general or firm-specific information that alters the market's expectations about the cash returns from current and future assets. Previous research has strongly supported the notion that the market efficiently incorporates new, publicly available information into stock prices. Therefore, when companies announce new strategic undertakings, their stock prices will adjust rapidly to reflect the expected risk and return consequences of these decisions.

There are three hypotheses that attempt to explain the stock market's reaction to announcements of corporate investment decisions. The "rational expectations" hypothesis, based on the economic theory of perfect competition, predicts no stock price reaction to corporate investments because investors expect managers to undertake periodic investments to maintain their firms' competitive fitness. The "institutional investors" hypothesis predicts a negative reaction to announcements of corporate investments. According to this hypothesis, the U.S. capital markets are dominated by institutional investors who, in pursuit of superior quarterly performance, look unfavorably on long-run investments because they reduce short-run profitability. The "shareholder value maximization" hypothesis predicts a positive reaction to corporate investments because the stock market rewards managers for developing corporate strategies that increase shareholder wealth.

Conventional wisdom, promulgated by the business press, typically supports the institutional investors hypothesis. Conversely, empirical research, though limited in quantity and scope, tends to support the shareholder value maximization hypothesis. The aforementioned study is the largest and most comprehensive of its kind, and therefore represents the best test yet of whether or not the stock market is an obstacle to long-run managerial decision making.

Study and Results

To examine the relationship between investment announcements and stock prices, a sample of corporate investment decisions was developed from articles that appeared in the *Wall Street Journal* during the period June 1972 to December 1987. This 15-year span showed substantial variation in economic activity and stock market behavior. The "What's News" column of the paper was surveyed for announcements that described corporate investment decisions, specifically those pertaining to the following items:

1. Joint venture formation (joint R&D project, shared assets, and asset construction)
2. R&D projects (new and ongoing)
3. Capital expenditures (plant modernization/capacity expansion and capital budget increase)
4. Product/market diversification (old product/new market, new product/old market, and new product/new market)

If an announcement was found in the "What's News" column, the full article was consulted to confirm the type of investment decision and to obtain additional information such as the size and expected duration of the investment.

The impact of an announcement on the value of the firm's common stock was assessed by measuring the differences between the actual and expected returns on the stock using an analytic method called the market-adjusted returns approach. The difference between the actual and the expected return (the later being an average computed for the S&P [Standard & Poor's] 500) is called the "excess" or "abnormal" return. The cumulative abnormal return over the "announcement period" (the day of the announcement in the *Wall Street Journal* and the prior trading day on the stock exchange) represents the market value that can be attributed directly to the announcement of the investment decision.

Effects of Corporate Announcements on Stock Prices

As shown in section A of Table A-1, the cumulative abnormal return during the announcement period for all 767 investment decisions was 0.64 percent. For all investment decisions, these two-day excess returns were by far the largest over the entire two-week period. In practical terms, a 0.64 percent abnormal return represents an effective annual return in excess of the overall market's performance of 220 percent. Stated differently, a 0.64 percent abnormal return for a large company with a market value of, say, $25 billion results in an increase in market value (adjusted for overall market movements) of $160 million in two days.

As indicated in section B of Table A-1, the cumulative abnormal returns of announcements regarding joint ventures and R&D projects were higher than the returns associated with capital expenditures and product/market diversification (0.80 percent and 1.13 percent versus 0.36 percent and 0.69 percent, respectively). One could argue that the stock market reacted most favorably to the riskiest and most uncertain of corporate investments in that the outcomes of joint ventures and R&D projects are harder to predict than those associated with capital expenditures and product/market diversification. Thus, both the overall results of the study and those associated with specific types of investment decisions strongly support the shareholder value maximization hypothesis. That is, when corporations that were part of the study announced their strategic investment decisions, the stock market usually reacted quickly and positively.

Table A-1. Strategic Investment Announcements and Stock Returns

	Day	Mean unadjusted return (R)	Percent unadjusted return greater than zero	Mean abnormal return (AR)	T-test (T)	Cumulative abnormal return (CAR)
		Section A. Overall Results				
All investment announcements (n=767)	-1	0.38	48.01	0.30	3.46†	0.30
	0	0.35	51.74	0.35	4.55°	0.64†
		Section B. Specific Types of Investment Announcements				
Joint venture (n=197)	-1	0.55	50.25	0.42	2.45†	0.42
	0	0.40	52.79	0.38	2.17*	0.80
R&D project (n=52)	-1	0.90	53.85	0.80	2.36†	0.80
	0	0.43	46.15	0.33	1.34	1.13
Capital expenditure (n=277)	-1	0.12	41.52	0.06	0.38	0.06
	0	0.23	50.54	0.31	2.64†	0.36
Product/market diversification (n=241)	-1	0.43	51.87	0.33	2.41†	0.33
	0	0.41	52.70	0.35	2.59†	0.69

*$p < 0.05$.
†$p < 0.01$.

Whereas investors usually responded positively to corporate investment announcements, they reacted negatively in some cases. It is speculated that the stock market may have lacked confidence in those firms' strategies or future prospects, their managers' ability to implement investment project successfully, or the timing of the proposed investments. Thus, it appears that the market attempted to differentiate between good and bad investment decisions; it did not behave monolithically.

Size and Duration Effects

For some of the investment announcements, information was available on the size of the investment or its expected duration. To incorporate investment size into the analysis, the dollar amount of the investment was first divided by the firm's total assets so that each investment was expressed as a relative percentage. Then the subsample of 365 investment announcements was dichotomized at the median, 5.3 percent. This permitted the assessments of stock market reaction to announcements of small versus large investments (i.e., less than or greater than 5.3 percent of total firm assets).

The expected life span of a corporate investment was provided in 287 cases. This subsample was divided into two categories, short-run (less than three years) and long-run (more than three years), and the stock market valuation of each group was calculated. It should be noted that in both the size and duration subsamples, more than 95 percent of the investments came from the R&D and capital expenditures categories. Very few joint venture diversification announcements contained size and duration information.

As shown in Table A-2, the two-day cumulative abnormal returns for small and large investments were virtually identical (0.47 percent and 0.46 percent, respectively). Long-run investments produced substantially greater returns than short-run investments (0.59 percent versus 0.23 percent). Both sets of returns represented significant increases in the market value of the firm. These results provided additional support for the shareholder value maximization hypothesis and clearly refuted the institutional investors hypothesis.

Table A-2. Size and Duration of Strategic Investment Announcements and Stock Returns

Day	Mean unadjusted return (R)	Percent unadjusted return greater than zero	Mean abnormal return (AR)	T-test (T)	Cumulative abnormal return (CAR)
		Section A. Investment Size			
Small (n=183)					
−1	0.17	43.2	0.11	0.84	0.11
0	0.33	50.3	0.37	2.95†	0.47
Large (n=182)					
−1	0.16	42.3	0.12	0.58	0.12
0	0.28	51.7	0.34	2.14*	0.46
		Section B. Investment Duration			
Short (n=194)					
−1	−0.02	43.3	−0.04	−0.22	−0.04
0	0.16	47.4	0.26	1.90*	0.23
Long (n=93)					
−1	0.16	41.9	0.13	0.69	0.13
0	0.31	52.7	0.46	2.21*	0.59

*$p<0.05$.
†$p<0.01$.

Conclusions

The result of this study has several important implications for strategic decision makers.

1. In contrast to the view of the business press, it appears that managers of successful companies need not worry about the stock market as they formulate corporate and business strategies. As evidenced in the diverse array of industries and companies examined in this study, announcements of corporate investments—including large, long-run investment projects—created, on average, substantial value for stockholders. Managers cannot ignore the market's expectations of short-run strategies aimed only at generating profits.

2. The stock market seems to favor announcements regarding investments in research and development and joint ventures over those in product/market diversification and capital expenditure. This suggests that the market may be in favor of lowering mobility barriers among firms because these forms of investment often involve alliances with other companies, including domestic or foreign competitors. Traditional business strategy has been predicated largely on how firms within an industry should attempt to erect mobility barriers to achieve competitive advantage over their rivals. Managers have been encouraged to understand how firms in their strategic group operate and to read the signals and moves of firms in other strategic groups. In the future, managers may be able to generate greater returns by developing collective strategies, network organizations, and other corporate alliances that compete in nontraditional ways.

3. It may appear at first glance that corporate strategists could make an investment announcement merely to increase a firm's market value and then not implement the decision. Whereas this study only evaluated the immediate stock price impact of corporate announcements, management's performance over time is a major factor in investors' assessments of future strategic directions and objectives. Therefore, any attempt to manipulate the market in this manner seems potentially unwise.

4. Today's corporate strategists face a considerable challenge in that they must meet the demands of a wide variety of con-

stituents. One very important constituent, of course, is the stock market, and we have shown that it does not penalize managers for making well-conceived, long-run strategic decisions. In fact, it rewards them for doing so. Moreover, the stock market does not appear to be an obstacle to meeting other constituents' needs, such as those of customers and employees. In the future, strategists should view the stock market as a valuable partner in the overall management of corporate enterprise.

About the Author

Michel (Mike) Robert is the founder of Decision Processes
International, Inc., a worldwide consulting firm, based in
Westport, Connecticut, with 60 partners in 15 countries.
Mr. Robert is the author of *The Strategist CEO: How Visionary
Executives Build Organizations* and *The Essence of Leadership:
Strategy, Innovation, and Decisiveness.* He is coauthor (with
Alan Weiss) of *The Innovative Formula: How Successful
Companies Turn Change into Opportunities.*

Index

Note: An *f*. after a page number refers to a figure; an *n*. refers to a note.